GOD
and ME

GOD

and ME

LYNETTE HARRIS DENTON

AMBASSADOR INTERNATIONAL
GREENVILLE, SOUTH CAROLINA & BELFAST, NORTHERN IRELAND

www.ambassador-international.com

God and Me

ISBN: 978-1-64960-311-1
eISBN: 978-1-64960-333-3

Cover Design by Hannah Linder Designs
Interior Typesetting by Dentelle Design
Edited by Martin Wiles

AMBASSADOR INTERNATIONAL
Emerald House
411 University Ridge, Suite B14
Greenville, SC 29601
United States
www.ambassador-international.com

AMBASSADOR BOOKS
The Mount
2 Woodstock Link
Belfast, BT6 8DD
Northern Ireland, United Kingdom
www.ambassadormedia.co.uk

The colophon is a trademark of Ambassador, a Christian publishing company.

Contents

Jesus in the Gym

"For we do not wrestle against flesh and blood, but against principalities, against powers, against the rulers of the darkness of this age, against spiritual hosts of wickedness in the heavenly places" (Eph. 6:12).

READ: EPHESIANS 6:12-19

A total workout starts with the soul. Training for life begins with our minds fixed on God. The gym shapes us with a body that screams, "Mercy!"

Yet, the battle rages in the spiritual arena, and God is the Iron Man Who puts a stranglehold on the defeated enemy. Satan is no match for God, our powerful Creator and Sustainer of life. So, power up for ultimate spiritual victory.

Satan and his team of evil misfits can do significant damage only if we fail to defend ourselves. Ephesians 6:10-11, 14-17 says:

> Finally, my brethren, be strong in the Lord and in the power of His might. Put on the whole armor of God, that you may be able to stand against the wiles of the devil . . . Stand therefore, having girded your waist with truth, having put on the breastplate of righteousness, and having shod your feet with the preparation of the gospel of peace; above all, taking the shield of faith with which you will be able to quench all the fiery darts of the wicked one. And take the helmet of salvation, and the sword of the Spirit, which is the word of God.

The breastplate of righteousness is right standing with God. Peace with the Lord comes from forgiveness of sins through faith in Jesus. This forgiveness gives us access to God through Jesus. The shield of faith helps us quench the enemy's fiery darts. "So then faith comes by hearing, and hearing by the word of God" (Rom. 10:17).

We build spiritual muscles by reading God's Word and meditating on it. The helmet of salvation comes when we accept Jesus as our Savior, placing our trust in Him as the payment for our sin. And the sword of the Spirit is the Word of God. So, immerse yourself in the Word daily. Power up with this full armor of God so that you realize ultimate victory, which saves to the uttermost.

THOUGHT FOR THE DAY
God is the undisputed Victor, and Satan is defeated.

PRAYER
Heavenly Father, help me build stronger muscles in my spiritual life so I might be a champion in my faith walk. In Jesus' name, amen.

Launch

"Then we who are alive and remain shall be caught up together with them in the clouds to meet the Lord in the air. And thus we shall always be with the Lord" (1 Thess. 4:17).

READ: 1 THESSALONIANS 4:14-17

If you've been on this earth for the past several decades, you may recall a song entitled "I'll Fly Away," a hymn written in 1929 by Albert E. Brumley and published in 1932. It expresses the beautiful hope of eternal life in Heaven.

While birds have an advantage over terrestrial creatures because they can fly, we humans must be content to move with bodily limitations. Birds simply fly away when threatened by a predator. This is a simple fact of life and how God designed it.

Someday, we will shout and sing with the angel band when the countdown starts and lift-off begins. As we "fly away" through space to our forever home, believers will rejoice at the prospect of an eternity of love, peace, and joy. On that day, we will delight in the love, safety, and protection of our Lord. No more needling from dark forces or evil powers. We will be safe in the arms of a loving Savior. Comfort, peace, joy, and love beyond our wildest imagination. No more struggles, temptations, pain, fear, corruption, curse, or death. Satan will be destroyed and cast into the lake of fire and brimstone. We will shout "Hallelujah" to the King of kings and Lord of lords: Jesus our Savior.

Revelation 21:3-4 tells us about our future home in Heaven. "And I heard a loud voice from heaven saying, 'Behold, the tabernacle of God *is* with men, and He will dwell with them, and they shall be His people. God Himself will be with them *and be* their God. And God will wipe away every tear from their eyes; there shall be no more death, nor sorrow, nor crying. There shall be no more pain, for the former things have passed away.'" Our reward for a faithful life awaits us in our eternal home.

THOUGHT FOR THE DAY
Someday, God will take away our sorrow. He will dwell with us and be our God. Believers will bask in the glory of the King—our Deliverer, our Savior, Jesus Christ.

PRAYER
Lord, prepare me for the day when I will leave earth and fly into the arms of a loving God. Remind me that it will be worth it when I reach my heavenly home and see You waiting for me. I eagerly long for that day when You reach out to me in infinite love and mercy. Nothing on this earth compares to what awaits me in Heaven. You await me, Lord, and I thank You for that hope. In Jesus' name, amen.

Lightning in a Bottle

"His body was like beryl, his face like the appearance of lightning, his eyes like torches of fire, his arms and feet like burnished bronze in color, and the sound of his words like the voice of a multitude" (Dan. 10:6).

READ: DANIEL 10:5-14

Billed as the most significant two minutes in sports, the Kentucky Derby is the most famous horse race in the world. Winners take away a minimum purse of two million dollars. Every jockey dreams of winning the most prestigious horse race of all time. Jockey Gary Stevens, a three-time winner of the coveted title, said, "Everybody wants to feel that lightning in a bottle." But, he added, "You can't really explain it unless you have experienced it."

That lightning in a bottle strikes the individual on a spiritual level when one accepts Jesus Christ as their personal Savior. However, this spiritual lightning can't be contained in a bottle but explodes into the everyday life of a believer with an unprecedented magnitude of force when lived out in a relationship with Almighty God, Jesus Christ, and the Holy Spirit. It manifests in love, joy, and "peace . . . which surpasses all understanding" (Phil. 4:7).

The relationship begins when we accept Jesus Christ as Savior. Then it matures as we produce the fruit of the Spirit: love, joy, peace, longsuffering, gentleness, goodness, faith, meekness, and temperance (Gal. 5:22-23). Gone are the days of uncertainty and doubt. God's forgiveness and love replace them.

Owning the love and trust in God's redemption through Christ's death, burial, and resurrection marks our journey in a way no other event can. We experience salvation on a level that defies description. For some, it begins like a burst of energy in the soul that spans into eternity. Others ignite slowly, like a smoldering fire that consumes us with a drive and desire for God.

Our Heavenly Father works with us individually in unique ways that match our distinctive nature. He accomplishes and completes a Divine design in us, which is influenced by our personality and passions, time and talents, and abilities and opportunities.

THOUGHT FOR THE DAY

Our days commence from Christ's sacrifice for us on Calvary's cross. Our choice to reject or receive Him determines our eternity. Matthew 27:50-54 tells how Christ crossed the finish line and began a new mile marker for humanity when He gave His life. My life has a new beginning because of Christ's overcoming victory. I am victorious when I place my life in His hands, trusting Him to deliver me.

PRAYER

Lord, thank You for winning the race, overcoming Satan, and providing salvation for those who trust in You. In Jesus' name, amen.

Merging with the Miraculous

"How God anointed Jesus of Nazareth with the Holy Spirit and with power: who went about doing good and healing all who were oppressed by the devil, for God was with Him" (Acts 10:38).

READ: ACTS 10:34-43

Healing? Where does it come from? Who gives the signal to heal? Who or what is the source of healing? Is it from the hospitals, clinics, nurses, and doctors? Are the pills in our medicine cabinets the source?

All of these encompass physical healing of a sort. But I am speaking of Divine healing—the kind that only comes from one source: God. Jesus said, "'God is not the God of the dead but of the living'" (Matt. 22:32). Once our lives are over and the coroner says we're dead, do miracles cease? Not when the Son of God calls us out of the grave as He did with Lazarus (John 11:43-44). Jesus also commanded the son of a widow to rise as he was being carried away in a funeral procession (Luke 7:12-15).

Divine miracles, indeed. According to Jesus' description, "'*the* blind see, *the* lame walk, *the* lepers are cleansed, *the* deaf hear, *the* dead are raised, *the* poor have the gospel preached to them'" (Luke 7:22). What mighty works of an awesome God! No mere acts of a weak nature, but God-empowered miracles.

Believers should merge our lives with the past actions of Jesus Christ. Miracles did not end with the conclusion of the last word of the Bible. Miracles are still a real possibility in our century. Putting our faith and trust in a God of limitless, infinite power pushes our ordinary life into the extra-ordinary—not simply extra-ordinary but supernatural.

As in traffic, merge your life into that of God's Divine possibilities and believe in the reality that our Creator lives. Christ encouraged us to be like Him. "'Most assuredly, I say to you, he who believes in Me, the works that I do he will do also; and greater *works* than these he will do, because I go to my Father'" (John 14:12).

THOUGHT FOR THE DAY

Living out my faith in God, I merge my ways with God's when I demonstrate my trust in His Divine nature.

PRAYER

Lord, I refuse to limit You with my perimeters. Instead, I believe and trust You for Divine miracles that You demonstrated when You walked on earth. These miracles may be displayed through You as I lean on You to deliver miraculously. I merge my will with Yours. Help me be ready and willing to submit to You so that You may demonstrate Your great power and love. You are our source of miracles. Only You can heal and help us by whatever methods You choose. In Jesus' name, amen.

I Am Who I Am

"And God said to Moses, 'I AM WHO I AM.' And He said, 'Thus you shall say to the children of Israel, I AM has sent me to you'" (Exod. 3:14).

READ: EXODUS 3:1-15

My cousin loaned me the Moses basket in which I carried my newborn son. She had carried her new baby in the wicker basket years earlier. Placing my infant son in the basket, I imagined how Moses' mother must have felt when she set him adrift on the Nile River in a reed basket. The basket I placed my tiny son in didn't need to float; it traveled safely only to church and back, and little more.

The account of Moses had a much graver history. Pharaoh told the Hebrew midwives to kill all the baby sons at birth. But the midwives, fearing God, refused to obey the king of Egypt. Concerned for her son, Moses' mother hid him for three months. Realizing she could no longer hide him, she made an ark of bulrushes, daubed it with a type of asphalt and pitch, put Moses in it, and placed it among the reeds by the riverbank.

When Pharaoh's daughter came to bathe in the river, she saw the ark in the water and took the baby for her own. Moses spent his days in Pharaoh's palace. Yet, when he was grown, he fled from Pharaoh, fearing for his life.

Years later, Moses delivered the Hebrew slaves out of the hands of the Egyptians, but it took some persuasion from God before he was up to the task. "But Moses said to God, 'Who *am* I that I should go to Pharaoh, and that I should bring the children of Israel out of Egypt'" (Exod. 3:11). Although Moses was raised in Egypt's royal palace, he hesitated when the Lord called him. God needed a robust and able leader to lead the Hebrews out of bondage.

God told Moses He would be with him. That's a confidence-builder. To know God is backing us gives confidence and strength like nothing else. With God on our side, we cannot fail. Knowing that was all Moses needed. When he wanted to know how to identify God to the children of Israel, God told him to say "I AM" had sent him.

THOUGHT FOR THE DAY
When God calls, He equips.

PRAYER
Heavenly Father, help me know the strength that comes only from You. Help me realize I can do whatever You ask when I rely on You. In Jesus' name, amen.

Little Is Much

"For they all put in out of their abundance, but she out of her poverty put in all that she had, her whole livelihood" (Mark 12:44).

READ: MARK 12:41-44

The devoted husband gave his faithful wife a small, unpretentious gift wrapped in brown paper. Inside the tiny box was a beautiful ring set with diamonds, rubies, and emeralds—a token of his love. Although a small package, it contained a precious gift. The size of the box did not represent the value of the present.

Little is much when God is in it, just as it was with the widow who gave from her lack. The offering she gave, although small, was significant. In contrast, Jesus observed many others fill the till in the sanctuary with lavish wealth. Although meager, the widow's two mites were all she had. What a grand gesture of love and sacrifice and a true spirit of generosity. No gift is greater than giving all we have, whether that all is little or much. The gift that consists of all we own is the greatest gift we can offer.

When we offer all we have, we give to God generously. The little we share is much when we share with a sincere heart and in appreciation for all He has done for us. God blesses those who give to Him, whether our gifts entail time, resources, talent, or money. He also recognizes the depth of the gift. A sacrificial offering reaches beyond mere mathematics. We can't out-give God.

We may not realize the returns on our investment in God's kingdom in monetary terms, although we may see that, too. God may reward with other blessings that are equally, or more, valuable—such things as good health, peace of mind, a solid marriage, or a joyful life. God doesn't forget those who honor Him with their resources. It's not a matter of money for money, as if God is the great slot machine in the sky. God may bless us with less-tangible gifts such as salvation, healing, and love. God meets our needs when we honor Him with our giving.

THOUGHT FOR THE DAY
Little is much when God is in it.

PRAYER
Lord, help me to give, even though it may be negligible. Help me remember that however small, it is much when I do it for Your glory. In Jesus' name, amen.

Lavish

"In Him we have redemption through His blood, the forgiveness of sins, according to the riches of His grace" (Eph. 1:7).

READ: EPHESIANS 1:7-9

Who is the wealthiest person in the world? It depends on when we ask that question since it changes periodically. We could be looking at one of the richest people on earth when we look into the mirror. When saved by the grace of God and living for Him, we are among the wealthiest on planet Earth. Our treasures may not be the gold and silver of this world, but we have true riches because we know Jesus as our Savior.

The love of God reaches beyond our finite dimensions of time and space. His love transcends our artificial boundaries. Proof of the love of God is manifest throughout Scripture.

John 3:16-17 assures us of God's love. "For God so loved the world that He gave His only begotten Son, that whoever believes in Him should not perish but have everlasting life. For God did not send His Son into the world to condemn the world, but that the world through Him might be saved."

Jesus' blood redeems us. Our efforts to save ourselves will fail. We can never be good enough, rich enough, or intelligent enough to merit salvation. If we attempt to set ourselves up as our Savior, we will discredit the grace of God. Finite and inadequate, we humans can never achieve what God freely gives us now and in eternity. God saves us through belief in His Son, Jesus. We have untold riches all because of God's grace.

THOUGHT FOR THE DAY
Seek God for Who He is, not for what He can do for you. Seek the Giver—not the gift.

PRAYER
Dear Heavenly Father, thank You for providing abundant grace and mercy. Your lavish gift of salvation reaches the expanse of my greatest needs. In Jesus' name, amen.

Are You Thirsty?

"Blessed are those who hunger and thirst for righteousness, For they shall be filled" (Matt. 5:6).

READ MATTHEW 5:3-10

While in college, I once ran out of gas. I'm not sure whether it was because I was irresponsible or because my car had no low fuel indicator light, but my 1966 Oldsmobile convertible refused to go another inch. That was over forty years ago, and I haven't run out of gas again.

But I have run out of gas spiritually. Just as my car was thirsty for the liquid that accelerated it, my soul thirsts after things that nourish my spirit. I desire to know God's will and live a life pleasing to Him. I want to live Romans 12:2: "And do not be conformed to this world, but be transformed by the renewing of your mind, that you may prove what is that good and acceptable and perfect will of God." I continually need to refuel spiritually.

As a young college student, I may have been ignorant about my gas level. However, I have learned that my needs go unsatisfied when I am spiritually empty. Impoverished and lacking, I become aware of my need for the touch of God. I become diligent in feeding my soul through prayer and meditation on God's Word. With a genuine spirit, I renew my commitment to Him. As I prioritize God, my hunger and thirst for righteousness are filled.

THOUGHT FOR THE DAY

As I awake to my constant need for God, He richly provides when I seek His face.

PRAYER

Heavenly Father, knowing I will someday give an account to You, help me live each day for You. In Jesus' name, amen.

Laboring Long

"For you remember, brethren, our labor and toil; for laboring night and day, that we might not be a burden to any of you, we preached to you the gospel of God" (1 Thess. 2:9).

READ: 1 THESSALONIANS 2:8-9

Remember when . . . ? Have you ever played the game? It tests the memory of the person with whom we are chatting. Remember when . . . we built a doghouse, made a go-kart, flew over the Grand Canyon. Sparking the memory with a test of "remember when" can be fun and can reinforce our past by helping us remember.

Paul stirred the memory of the Thessalonians, charging them to remember the long hours he had worked. He had labored long so he would not burden them financially while he was busy relaying the Gospel message. Lest they were tempted to accuse him of laziness while supporting him, Paul reminded them of the long hours he had spent making tents.

Paul was genuine in his drive to preach the Gospel. He was willing to work while he worshiped, sharing the good news of salvation through Jesus Christ. He was not looking for an easy way of life.

We sometimes find charlatans who use the pulpit for material gain. The name-it-claim-it crowd assumes God is the great slot machine in the sky, Who dispenses riches to those who sit on His lap, mouthing their wish list to him as a child does to Santa. God is not interested in being a partner to anyone who uses Him for their gain or to set up a memorial to themselves. If our love for and dedication to God is not genuine, if we are in it for only what we can get out of it, if we pollute our service with impure motives, then we endanger our spiritual posture. 1 Corinthians 3:13-15 reads, "Each one's work will become clear; for the Day will declare it, because it will be revealed by fire; and the fire will test each one's work, of what sort it is. If anyone's work which he has built on *it* endures, he will receive a reward. If anyone's work is burned, he will suffer loss; but he himself will be saved, yet so as through fire."

THOUGHT FOR THE DAY

It may be tempting to further my cause, but no sacrifice is too large or small when I promote the Kingdom of God with sincerity and love.

PRAYER

Lord, help me calculate my motives, counting it all worthy to be used by You for the sake of the Gospel of Jesus Christ. In Jesus' name, amen.

Keeping Good Company

"Do not be deceived: 'Evil company corrupts good habits'" (1 Cor. 15:33).

READ: 1 CORINTHIANS 15:30-34

We're all familiar with the adage, "Birds of a feather flock together." We don't see the hummingbird soaring with the eagle or the sparrow making its nest among the marshes with the wood duck. Birds stay with those that share their nature. The brightly colored parrots of the Amazon share their habitat with other parrots like themselves in the rainforest. The Canadian goose would be out of place in such extreme heat. Birds of like nature do, indeed, flock together.

Likewise, the believer who wants to stay close to God shares fellowship with like-minded believers. Sharing life's experiences with those who believe as we do can build our faith. When doubt surfaces, a fellow Christian can encourage us in the faith. When trials assail us, a godly person can support us. When hardships pound us, we can find comfort from a righteous person. In addition, the joy of knowing Christ makes us want to share that joy with others. God's love multiplies as we spread it to others who believe.

We sometimes assimilate the habits of others. We adapt to their way of acting, imitating their style of behavior. Therefore, it is essential to choose friends who live for the Lord. They can help us in our journey. Righteous habits at times produce a copycat behavior in other believers. As we pursue commitment to God, other members of the body of Christ may duplicate godly living. On the other hand, sin and immorality destroy our relationship with God. When morality takes a nose-dive, others can fall along with us. Evil company corrupts even the best.

Watch with whom you run. Keep company with others who live godly lives. Shun all appearance of evil. Build yourself up with good company.

THOUGHT FOR THE DAY
Avoid evil and cherish your friendship with fellow believers.

PRAYER
Heavenly Father, make me aware of my place in You, so I choose to do the right thing. Help me to surround myself with people who love and honor You. In Jesus' name, amen.

Anyone Who Will Listen

"So then faith comes by hearing, and hearing by the word of God" (Rom. 10:17).

READ: ROMANS 10:13-17

When doing wrong, children may hear a parent ask after correcting them, "Do you hear me?" The question doesn't concern sound waves reaching the ears of the little one. Instead, it entails recognizing the meaning of what they say. After committing a misdeed, another phrase the parent might ask is, "Do you understand?" This question seeps deeper into the psyche by examining comprehension. If the child understands, the parent might also say, "I don't want to tell you again."

Although we understand many lessons, we often repeat mistakes and suffer the consequences. The Lord gives us His Word to guide, correct, encourage, and express His love for us—actually, to save us. "Faith *comes* by hearing, and hearing by the word of God" (Rom. 10:17). Pouring God's Word into our souls and following those words lead us in the right direction—God's direction. We can minimize our suffering, discomfort, and pain by accepting God's Word and living by it. Doing so ensures spiritual growth.

THOUGHT FOR THE DAY
Am I hearing the Word of God?

PRAYER
Dear Heavenly Father, please open my ears to hear and know Your spiritual truth. May I tell others about You so they may hear Your Word. Increase my faith. In Jesus' name, amen.

Transformation

· "And do not be conformed to this world, but be transformed by the renewing of your mind, that you may prove what is that good and acceptable and perfect will of God" (Rom. 12:2).

READ: ROMANS 12:1-3

My young son and I toyed with a child's craft project known as "Shrinky Dinks," which requires putting the project in the oven and watching it shrink. It comes out looking nothing like the object placed there only moments earlier. The heat from the oven shrinks the art and transforms it as if by magic. It's fun and exciting to see the artwork changed.

Much like the art project, we undergo spiritual transformation when we renew our minds with the Word of God and prayer. Profound study and meditation on Scripture immerse us in God's will and ways. A seasoned believer who effectively lives a godly life has spent considerable time studying the Word. However, brief exposure does not fill us with deep knowledge and understanding of God's will. Only then can we apply what we know so that our actions are a living testimony of God's Divine will.

Prayer is putting our thoughts into words, whether silently or audibly, so that we have a connection with our Divine Creator. Prayer must be two-way communication to be effective. Not only do we relate our thoughts to God, but we also listen for His still, small voice. A monologue is a simple discourse originating from one person. But conversation is an exchange of ideas from both parties. We express our thoughts to God and expect His input. If we slow down and listen intently, we recognize His voice as He speaks to our inner being.

THOUGHT FOR THE DAY
A complete connection with our Creator requires prayer and meditation on the Bible.

PRAYER
Lord, slow me down enough to hear Your still, small voice speaking to me as I pray. Help me complete Your will in my life by studying Your Word so that I might apply it to my daily living. In Jesus' name, amen.

It Ain't for Sissies

"But even if you should suffer for righteousness' sake, you are *blessed. And do not be afraid of their threats, nor be troubled" (1 Peter 3:14).*

READ: 1 PETER 3:14-17

A friend reached Medicare age and was thrilled with receiving medical treatments at such a reasonable rate—until a physical malady struck. Suffering from an age-related sickness, someone jokingly said, "Growing old ain't for sissies."

How true. And we might add that being a Christian ain't for sissies either. Many believers are ridiculed for their faith. Some are tortured and even put to death. The trend toward tolerance seems to apply to all religions except Christianity. Believers are often accused of hating or being extremists when they oppose activities the Bible opposes. God wants us to be holy. He promises us an eternity with Him when we trust in Jesus. We don't need others' approval; we need only God's approval.

Knowing we may suffer for our beliefs requires strength. Others may threaten us, but God is on our side. "And do not fear those who kill the body but cannot kill the soul. But rather fear Him who is able to destroy both soul and body in hell" (Matt. 10:28). God rewards those who fear and honor Him, not others.

THOUGHT FOR THE DAY
Never submit to the fear of others. Instead, place your trust and confidence in God—the Keeper of your soul.

PRAYER
Lord, if I find myself caught up in fear, remind me that You are with me to the ends of the earth. Help me to realize there is nothing to fear when I put my trust in You. In Jesus' name, amen.

God Is Not Malicious

"As for God, His way is perfect; the word of the Lord is proven; He is a shield to all who trust in Him" (Psalms 18:30).

READ: PSALM 18:27-31

Albert Einstein, one of the greatest minds of his time, is credited with saying, "God is subtle, but He is not malicious."

God is good all the time. How precious is the Lord in His righteousness and justice. He is our refuge and stronghold in times of trouble. When we trust and put our confidence in Him, He saves us. He has mercy on the sinner and shows His steadfast love. Psalm 51:10 says, "Create in me a clean heart, O God, and renew a steadfast spirit within me." The Holy Spirit restored the joy of the psalmist's salvation.

God's lovingkindness makes my heart bubble over with thanks. I will praise and give Him thanks forever. "Great *is* the LORD, and greatly to be praised" (Psalm 145:3). We should offer God the sacrifice of praise, for He is our Redeemer.

I rely on the mercy of God, and my inner self thirsts for the living God. I hope in God and wait expectantly for Him. God is my Helper and Ally.

THOUGHT FOR THE DAY
God is good—even when I don't deserve His goodness.

PRAYER
God, thank You for Your love and kindness. Help me trust You in all things, even when I don't understand. In Jesus' name, amen.

Be Significant

"But you shall receive power when the Holy Spirit has come upon you; and you shall be witnesses to Me in Jerusalem, and in all Judea and Samaria, and to the end of the earth" (Acts 1:8).

READ: ACTS 1:7-8

Feeling worthless? Such was the attitude of a young boy whose parents had told him all his life that he wouldn't amount to anything. When he reached adulthood, he did poorly. Success for him meant being a failure—living up to his parents' expectations. Although deemed worthless by others, God valued him. He was loved and treasured by the Creator of the universe. God's love is so complete that "while we were still sinners," He sent His Son to die for us (Rom. 5:8).

Regardless of our station in life, we have value. Our Creator extends His love to us and has a vested interest in our lives. He is a caring God, ready to receive and rescue the most "worthless" of persons the world ignores.

We are unique and have something to offer that no other person can. We have a smile, a compliment, or a talent that is ours alone. God wants us to use this special uniqueness for Him. We can give from our hearts and bless others. We can use our traits to edify Christ so that we magnify the love of God to those we meet. Our godly actions declare God's love when we let our lights shine.

Acts 5:14-15 says, "Believers were increasingly added to the Lord, multitudes of both men and women, so that they brought the sick out into the streets and laid *them* on beds and couches, that at least the shadow of Peter passing by might fall on some of them."

Our lives should be a conduit for the outflow of Spirit-empowered love and forgiveness. It will when we display God's love in tangible ways. Start with faith. Then, pray and let God lead. Next, share the good news of God's love and forgiveness.

THOUGHT FOR THE DAY

Our footprint on this planet positively impacts us when we show God's love, mercy, and forgiveness.

PRAYER

Thank You, God, that Your Son embraced the lowest, the least, and the lost with overwhelming love and acceptance. Help me make an impact on those who are suffering. Help me become love in action. In Jesus' name, amen.

God's Covenant with Abraham

"And I will make My covenant between Me and you, and will multiply you exceedingly" (Gen. 17:2).

READ: GENESIS 17:1-13

What's in a name? We would find many entries if we looked up the name Smith in the phone book. It's a common name. Knowing this, a mother whose last name was Smith wanted to name her little girl something different. She chose Unique Smith. That name would stand out among all the Smiths of the world. Few girls, if any, had that name. Unique Smith was one of a kind—a name that conveyed individuality.

God thought the meaning of a name was significant when it related to Abraham and Sarah. At ninety-nine years old, the Lord made a covenant with Abram, promising him that he would become a mighty nation and that all the nations of the earth would be blessed in him. The Lord also announced, "No longer shall your name be called Abram, but your name shall be Abraham; for I have made you a father of many nations" (Gen. 17:5). And a few verses later, we read, "Then God said to Abraham, 'As for Sarai your wife, you shall not call her name Sarai, but Sarah *shall be* her name'" (Gen. 17:15).

Such a slight change in a name, but it was significant enough for God to deem it so. It marked a covenant relationship between Him and Abraham. Abraham's part in the covenant required every male child among his kin to be circumcised. God's everlasting covenant with Abraham was marked in the flesh for every male for generations to come. Also, God would bless Sarah with a son. She would be a mother of nations, kings, and peoples.

THOUGHT FOR THE DAY
God knows me by name. When I accept Jesus, there's a new name written down in the Book of Life.

PRAYER
Thank You, Lord, that my confession of faith in Jesus offers a new and better covenant.
In Jesus' name, amen.

In Your Prime

"Just as I was in the days of my prime, When the friendly counsel of God was over my tent; When the Almighty was yet with me, When my children were around me; When my steps were bathed with cream, And the rock poured out rivers of oil for me" (Job 29:4-6).

READ: JOB 29:1-20

Feeling bitter, disappointed, neglected, discouraged, or angry? Welcome to humanity. With enough time under our belts, all of us will experience some, if not all, of these emotions. Life is not all peaches and cream. Poverty strikes; marriages collapse; health fails; businesses go bankrupt; and dreams are dashed. We are cast into difficult situations that sometimes zap our physical and emotional strength. Opposition rears its head and strangles us with doubt, anxiety, and fear. Failure, loss, and disappointment run paramount.

How do we deal with such stressful situations when the chips are down? Do we turn from God, or do we run to Him? When circumstances are against us, we can choose to follow our reasoning, seek our solutions, blame God, or snatch victory from the hands of defeat by relying on God to move.

Trusting Him, acknowledging Him, obeying Him, submitting to Him, and surrendering to Him give us a jump-start on solving the problems we encounter and recovering from the disasters we face.

In the Old Testament, Job had lost everything of value—including his children, his health, his livestock, and his friends' support. He may have wondered what was left. In his prime, he had accumulated wealth and the support of his family and friends. Through all his afflictions, he questioned and considered his misfortune (Job 24). Yet Job said, "The Lord gave, and the Lord has taken away; Blessed be the name of the Lord" (Job 1:21). In the end, God restored Job's losses. As a result, Job concluded the Lord was worthy to be praised.

THOUGHT FOR THE DAY
The Lord works behind the scenes when we may be unaware of His mighty hand.

PRAYER
Lord, whether young or old, rich or poor, help me praise You in whatever state I am.
In Jesus' name, amen.

Your Worth in God

"I have seen all the works that are done under the sun; and indeed, all is vanity and grasping for the wind" (Eccl. 1:14).

READ: ECCLESIASTES 1:12-15

Our culture often values a woman for her beauty and a man for his wealth. What a poor standard. For those of us who are neither wealthy nor beautiful, we fail miserably according to that standard.

But God does not judge us by our beauty, wealth, education, career, IQ, weight, physical condition, social status, car, house, vacations, or any other measuring stick we might achieve. We find our worth in God, not human effort. Knowing this, we should dismiss our pride and humble ourselves. God uses only one criterion to judge us: our belief in Jesus Christ as our personal Savior and Lord.

We are not equal with God. He is the Master of the universe. We are His creation, and His assessment measures our worth. How valuable are we to Him? God sent His only begotten Son, Jesus, to die for us. "But God demonstrates His own love toward us, in that while we were still sinners, Christ died for us" (Rom. 5:8). This is a priceless value.

THOUGHT FOR THE DAY
My value is wrapped up in God, not my human worth.

PRAYER
Thank You, Lord, for loving me enough to send Your Son to die for me. You, and You only, validate my worth as an individual. In Jesus' name, amen.

How Long Is Long Enough?

"And Jesus said to him, 'Assuredly, I say to you, today you will be with Me in Paradise'" (Luke 23:43).

READ: LUKE 23:40-43

Six gold-glittered candles, jeweled pomegranates, and crystal vases captured the essence of the festive dinner table planned for the special occasion. The sparkling crystal and fine china graced the table with exceptional beauty. However, during preparations, one of the candles fell from its place and crashed to the floor. With time of the essence and the festivities quickly approaching, the hostess returned to the store to replace the broken candle.

When she couldn't purchase a matching candle, she returned the remaining candles for a refund. But when she asked for a refund, the salesclerk informed her the purchase had been made with a check and would require waiting seven days before she could receive her refund. A speedy reimbursement was out of the question.

Disappointed, the hostess chose another piece to enhance her elaborate table decorations. Although beautiful, it didn't quite deliver the same stunning effect the candles provided, but no time remained to make other plans for the party. Second-best would have to do.

Second-best should never be an option when it comes to our spiritual life. Instead, making choices that are in tune with God's plans for our lives should take priority. God's best for our life is assured when we consider Him in all we do. But how are we to know God's design for our life?

We can know the will of God when we search the Scriptures and pray about our circumstances. Additionally, wise counsel from those who have experienced life equips us to make better choices. Of utmost importance, we must listen intently to the direction of the Holy Spirit in situations where we might doubt our choices. When we allow the Holy Spirit to guide us, He will direct us in the right way. Doing so requires having an open heart and mind to follow His direction. Only then will God's best be evident in our life.

THOUGHT FOR THE DAY
Now is the best time to seek God.

PRAYER
Lord, make my life centered around Your will. Immediately seeking You assures me of wise choices. Second-best is not an option when You have Your way in my life. In Jesus' name, amen.

We Can't Exhaust God's Love

"But God demonstrates His own love toward us, in that while we were still sinners, Christ died for us" (Rom. 5:8).

READ: ROMANS 5:6-11

How much does God love me? Enough to give me air to breathe? Enough to give me life? Sufficient to provide me with eternity for my future? Just how much does God love me? Elizabeth Barrett Browning, an English poet in the Victorian era, composed a memorable line in a famous sonnet: "How do I love thee? Let me count the ways." She posed this line to her husband, the love of her life.

If we were to count the ways God loves us, we could go on and on. Trusting God's love might begin with the gift of life itself. Yet even before human life began, God prepared a universe full of wonders for this coming creation. Showing His love, God created the moon, stars, sun, planets, oceans, seas, lakes, trees, flowers for beauty and sweet perfume, and nature for all to enjoy—among the many other gifts He offers. God's bounty of blessings for His creation is plenteous. And yet His love doesn't stop there.

These multiple and magnificent gifts might seem like good behavior rewards, but they aren't. God's love radiates to the loveliest and kindest, as well as the basest and most vile. A beautiful face, a stately demeanor, a padded wallet, a certificate of education, a lavish home, or a prestigious automobile do not gain any more love from God.

God proved His love extends beyond our wildest imagination by sending His only begotten Son to die for us—while we were yet sinners. Jesus did not die for the lovely, the righteous, the excellent, or the noble. God sent His Son to die for the *sinner.* Loving someone who agrees with us, compliments us, or keeps up with our likes and preferences is easy. More difficult is loving those who do not conform to our value system. Loving the unlovable or the less desirable becomes a little challenging. Yet that is what God did for us. He loved us beyond measure when we were the most unlovable. When we smacked of sin and disgrace, God refused to close His heart and stop loving us. He sent His Son to redeem us because of His love.

THOUGHT FOR THE DAY
God sees His creation, though flawed with sin, and provides redemption for His children.

PRAYER
Thank You for loving me, despite my faults. Your love proves my worth. In Jesus' name, amen.

God Saw It Was Good

"Then God saw everything that He had made, and indeed it was very good. So the evening and the morning were the sixth day" (Gen. 1:31).

READ: GENESIS 1:1-31

"In the beginning, God created the heavens and the earth" (Gen. 1:1) in six days. On the seventh day, He rested from all his work. He blessed this day and sanctified it (Gen. 2:3).

On each of the six days, God created something unique. After each creation, He declared it was good. After God created light, He said it was good. God created the earth and the seas and proclaimed them good. The earth brought forth grass, herbs, and trees, and God said they were good. God made lights to shine by day and night (the sun, moon, and stars) and said they were good. After He made the fish of the sea and the birds of the air, God pronounced they were good.

When God made all the animals and things that creep on the earth, He declared that it was good. Saving the best for last, God created humans in His image. This time, He looked over His creation and saw it was very good.

THOUGHT FOR THE DAY
God made us in His image.

PRAYER
"Create in me a clean heart, O God," (Psalm 51:10) so that You might see me and say of Your creation, "It was very good." In Jesus' name, amen.

Whose Name Is Holy

"You shall not take the name of the Lord your God in vain, for the Lord will not hold him guiltless who takes His name in vain" (Exod. 20:7).

READ: EXODUS 20:1-17

A burglar once watched a man's house. Seeing the man leave in the middle of the day, the burglar slipped into the house. Looking around, he found many treasures for the taking. Putting some items into his bag, he heard a voice: "Jesus is going to get you." He stopped, but then heard the voice again: "Jesus is going to get you." The burglar saw a cage with a parrot in it. Relieved, he realized it was the parrot talking. No longer feeling alarmed, he started up the stairs. Halfway up, a fierce-looking Doberman confronted him. The Doberman growled and showed his teeth. The parrot said, "Meet Jesus."

While this is only a story, the name of Jesus is powerful and mighty. "Then the seventy returned with joy, saying, 'Lord, even the demons are subject to us in Your name'" (Luke 10:17). Jesus is the name above every other name in Heaven and on earth (Phil. 2:9).

Paul ascertains the power of that name in Ephesians 1:20-21. "Which He worked in Christ when He raised *Him* from the dead and seated Him at His right hand in the heavenly *places*, far above all principality and power and might and dominion, and every name that is named, not only in this age but also in that which is to come." Simply calling upon the name of Jesus stirs us to salvation. "And it shall come to pass, *That* whoever calls on the name of the Lord Shall be saved" (Acts 2:21).

Our Heavenly Father is righteous and pure, and His name is holy. When a disciple of Jesus asked how to pray, the Lord acknowledged the sacredness and purity of God's name. "So He said to them, 'When you pray, say: Our Father in heaven, Hallowed be Your name. Your kingdom come. Your will be done On earth as *it is* in heaven'" (Luke 11:2).

When contemplating the name of God and thinking about Him, we must honor His name. Likewise, in our conversations, keeping His name holy is important. Casually using slander when speaking of the Lord is disrespectful and dishonors His holy name. A holy God never accepts cursing in flippant conversations or serious dialogue.

THOUGHT FOR THE DAY
There is power in the name of God and His Son, Jesus.

PRAYER
Lord, make me mindful of Your righteousness as I honor You with godly speech. In Jesus' name, amen.

Imagine That

"Now faith is the substance of things hoped for, the evidence of things not seen" (Heb. 11:1).

READ: HEBREWS 11:1-3

Imagine you are the creator of a new blockbuster movie, a songwriter for a platinum record, the author of a best-selling book, or a designer for a spectacular theme park. Let your imagination run wild. On the other hand, pause for a moment and imagine what your greatest dream in the spiritual world would be. If your grandest prayers were answered, what would you pray? If you knew you could not fail, what would you ask of God? Imagine big. Don't limit yourself. And certainly, don't limit God. Make a list of what you want to see God accomplish through you.

Hebrews 11:1 tells us, "Now faith is the substance of things hoped for, the evidence of things not seen." It is the apparent evidence in real life of what we have imagined. It is the fleshed-out dream of what we want when praying and believing. Big prayers often get significant results. God is big enough to answer your prayers in a big way. We serve a limitless God.

Hebrews 11:3 says, "By faith we understand that the worlds were framed by the word of God, so that the things which are seen were not made of things which are visible." God spoke the world into existence. He created it all with His word. From nothing, He brought into being everything visible and invisible.

THOUGHT FOR THE DAY

God created and maintains everything. He can save, heal, and bring to life His creation.

PRAYER

Lord, may my faith grow so that Your great, generous, and gracious will predominates my life. Help me imagine Your will for my life and place that plan into action through faith in You. Although it might be hard, help me accomplish what You desire for me, one day at a time. In Jesus' name, amen.

Delightful

"Your word I have hidden in my heart, That I might not sin against You" (Psalm 119:11).

READ: PSALM 119:9–16

Buzzing through the sky toward my hummingbird feeder hanging from my back porch, the ruby-throated hummingbird chattered loudly over his find. With nothing in sight but the bird and the feeder, I wondered for whom this cheerful chatter was intended. It was as if he were rejoicing aloud over the sweet nectar, though all alone. It was as if he were laughing, "all the way to the bank." This was not a one-time occurrence but an every-time occurrence when approaching the feeder.

We learn in Psalm 1 that people who delight in the Word of God, meditating on His law day and night, will prosper. They are "like a tree Planted by the rivers of water, That brings forth its fruit" (Psalm 1:3). The tree has an abundant, almost limitless, water supply for its thirsty leaves.

Those who love God's Word should always desire His direction, guidance, and promises. The truths in the Bible are jewels of wisdom, promise, and good counsel.

THOUGHT FOR THE DAY
The Word of God is a shield to the believer who values the gems in its pages.

PRAYER
Heavenly Father, I give You controlling interest in my life as I meditate on Your Word, making it "a lamp to my feet And a light to my path" (Psalm 119:105). In Jesus' name, amen.

When Should We Stop Rejoicing

"Rejoice always" (1 Thess. 5:16).

READ: 1 THESSALONIANS 5:15-22

The teen years are awkward for many. I was no exception. As a teenager, I was timid. When our youth leader asked us to recite our favorite Bible verse, I staggered at the thought. Because of my timidity, I could only recite the brief verse found in John 11:35: "Jesus wept." It was the shortest verse I could recall in the entire Bible. But Paul's imperative to the Thessalonian believers is equally as short. Those dynamic words pack a punch. Rejoice or celebrate. If Paul were to tell us in the language of today, he might say, "Let's party."

Rejoice. Sing and shout the praises. Rejoice out loud. When things are looking up, rejoice. When we hear good news, rejoice. When we experience a great victory, rejoice.

What are we to do when life surrounds us with trials and tribulation? When life is full of heartache and sorrow, what then? Should we bury our heads in the pillow and retreat? Should we stop rejoicing in the Lord?

No, we should rejoice in all situations—positive and negative. When life is pleasant, rejoice. When life surrounds us with opposition, rejoice. We are encouraged to rejoice always.

Rejoicing is easy when circumstances go our way, but rejoicing can be difficult when the negative surrounds us. While we are not required to rejoice over life's tragedies, we are to rejoice during our trials. We should always rejoice in God's love, mercy, and goodness.

A good, loving, and merciful God stands alongside us to comfort and guide us. Although trials assail us, we can stand firm in His love. Rejoice that He will bring us through. He is waiting in the portals to comfort us. Rejoice always in God's unrelenting love.

THOUGHT FOR THE DAY

In trials or triumphs, God is always with me. Knowing He loves and cares for me is reason enough to rejoice in Him always.

PRAYER

Lord, Your love abounds when all else fails. Surround me with that love through the good times and the bad. I rejoice in Your presence, knowing You care for me. In Jesus' name, amen.

A Pure Heart

"Blessed are *the pure in heart, For they shall see God" (Matt. 5:8).*

READ: MATTHEW 5:7-9

"Sin City" boasts, "What happens in Vegas, stays in Vegas." Gambling, alcohol, strip clubs, indecent shows, brothels, and drugs corrupt this jazz-jaded society, making Sodom and Gomorrah look tame.

Believers are to be holy people. Second Corinthians 6:17 says, "'Come out from among them and be separate, says the Lord. Do not touch what is unclean, and I will receive you.'" Paul admonishes us to be a separate people. Although we are in the world, we are not of the world.

When my son was young, I encouraged him in prayer each night by imploring him to let God's Spirit help him shun all appearances of evil. I called on God on behalf of my son with earnest and sincere prayers, hoping he would make wise and godly choices.

Knowing the importance of holy living, we should make having a pure heart one of our top priorities. "Flee also youthful lusts; but pursue righteousness, faith, love, peace with those who call on the Lord out of a pure heart" (2 Tim. 2:22). Jesus promises that those who are pure in heart will see God. We can only imagine the joy when we come into His presence and see Him face to face.

THOUGHT FOR THE DAY
God wants us to be a separate people who have pure hearts.

PRAYER
Heavenly Father, create a pure heart in me so I might be acceptable to You. In Jesus' name, amen.

Worth It All

"Blessed are you when they revile and persecute you, and shall say all kinds of evil against you falsely for My sake" (Matt. 5:11).

MATTHEW 5:1-12

Youcef Nadarkhani, an Iranian pastor, was sentenced to death for converting to Christianity. Refusing to renounce Jesus, he was willing to die for his beliefs. Beatings, imprisonment, and the death penalty threaten some who claim Christ as their Savior.

John 7:13 shows that many people in Jesus' day would not speak openly about Him for fear of the Jews. Fear of attack by those in power spread throughout the region where Jesus taught the Gospel. Those in power, the Sanhedrin, opposed the Lord and sought to destroy Him. Jesus experienced persecution and ultimate death by the cross.

In Matthew 5:44, Jesus taught how people should behave toward persecution and violence. We are to "love [our] enemies, bless those who curse [us], do good to those who hate [us], and pray for those which spitefully use [us] and persecute [us]" (Matt. 5:44). Jesus implored us to turn the other cheek. Jesus' Sermon on the Mount in Matthew 5-7 describes the qualities of a true disciple.

THOUGHT FOR THE DAY
When I think others are mistreating me, remind me that it will be worth it all when I see Jesus.

PRAYER
Lord, help me show love and kindness when people oppose me for the Gospel's sake. Your example is proof that I should turn the other cheek. In Jesus' name, amen.

Whatcha Doing?

"Hatred stirs up strife, But love covers all sins" (Prov. 10:12).

READ: PROVERBS 10:12; 1 JOHN 4:7-10

The message on a bumper sticker read, "Women who behave never make history." Does that mean women who misbehave do make history? This tin-plate theology seems to applaud misbehavior. I was curious what the owner of the car had done to pay tribute to misconduct. Was it something as minor as throwing her gum out the window, chasing the cat with a broom, speeding through a no-passing zone, or something more horrendous that would pierce even the darkest soul?

Whatever our misdeeds, God waits to forgive those who have failed. And we all fail Him at various times throughout our life's journey—often many times. His love covers all sins—not just some, but all. Love steps up and forgives. And we learn in 1 John 4:8, "He who does not love does not know God, for God is love." We can't do anything that will make God stop loving us. Nothing. God desires our repentance. Whether a little sin or one that sends a person to death row, God forgives when we are genuinely sorry and ask Him with heartfelt repentance. When we repent, He forgives, "for God is love."

So, when we go out of bounds of the acceptable, we recover when we seek God's approval by asking for His forgiveness and turning from our sins to His righteousness. Being human makes us apt to sin since we are not perfect. And God knows our nature. He is ready to remedy our sinful nature and give the Spirit to lead and guide us. Although we are imperfect now, He offers forgiveness.

THOUGHT FOR THE DAY
There is nothing we can do that will stop God from loving us.

PRAYER
Heavenly Father, help me be sensitive to the Holy Spirit so I might not sin. Thank You that Your love covers my sins. In Jesus' name, amen.

Does It Get Any Better?

"Indeed, You have made my days as handbreadths, and my age is as nothing before You; Certainly every man at his best state is but vapor. Selah" (Psalm 39:5).

READ: PSALM 39:5-6

As the focus of tabloids, the Hollywood star reveled in delight with fame and fortune. Could life get any better? What more did she need or want? Yet something was missing. She longed for the undefined—peace, joy, love, and happiness. Success, however rewarding, did not bring her what she most desired. At her best, she knew life was but a vapor. And the glamor, riches, and fame were simply a misty fog. Real hope and true riches lay beyond her grasp.

God promises us residence in the New Jerusalem, which will descend out of Heaven from God and have His glory. The city's light will be like a precious stone, as clear as crystal. The city itself is pure gold, like transparent glass. And the twelve gates of the city are each made of pearls. The streets are pure gold, like transparent glass. This city does not need the sun or moon for the glory of God illuminates it, and the Lamb is the Light. Proceeding from the throne of God and the Lamb is a pure river of life—it, too, is as clear as crystal. In the middle of the main street and on either side of the river stands the tree of life, bearing twelve fruits. The leaves of the tree are for the healing of the nations. There shall be no more curse, but the throne of God and the Lamb shall be in it, and we shall serve Him (Rev. 21).

THOUGHT FOR THE DAY
It is genuinely unspeakable what the Lord has done.

PRAYER
Lord, thank You for Your incredible gift that awaits us in eternity. Your reward gives us the right to the tree of life in that city where You tabernacle with us. In Jesus' name, amen.

Turn Dreams into Reality

"We are hard-pressed on every side, yet not crushed; we are perplexed, but not in despair; persecuted, but not forsaken; struck down, but not destroyed" (2 Cor. 4:8-9).

READ: 2 CORINTHIANS 4:6-12

A strong weight pressed down the steel, yet did not crush it. Instead, the steel only became stronger. The swaying palm trees bent over in the strong hurricane winds but did not break. Instead, they had sprung back to their upright position once the winds abated. Perplexed that he hadn't passed the difficult math test, the student did not despair. Instead, he determined to study and do better the next time. Persecuted for her faith in God, the struggling refugee continued to believe and serve the Lord.

Difficulties abound throughout our lives—tests, trials. No one gets by without stretching their endurance, patience, and mental and physical strength.

Are you in that uncomfortable, perhaps even critical, zone where the world seems to be crashing down upon you? Does your head ache from the pressures surrounding you? Do your shoulders sag under the weight of your problems? If so, you are not alone. Jesus is there to bear your burdens for you. We do not have to carry them by ourselves. Psalm 91:1-2 tells us, "He who dwells in the secret place of the Most High shall abide under the shadow of the Almighty. I will say of the Lord, *'He is* my refuge and my fortress; My God, in Him I will trust.'"

What is this secret place? It is the protection and comfort we find when we place our lives in God's hands. It is the time and place where God can heal and protect us from all harm when we trust Him.

THOUGHT FOR THE DAY
Crashing around me, the storms of life charge toward me with a fierce force, but the Lord God is my Refuge and Strength in my time of need.

PRAYER
Heavenly Father, thank You for shielding, protecting, and comforting me in life's storms. In Jesus' name, amen.

Holy, Holy, Holy

"And one cried to another and said: 'Holy, holy, holy is the Lord of hosts; the whole earth is full of His glory'" (Isa. 6:3).

READ: ISAIAH 6:1-4

"Is there a doctor in the house?" We've all heard the cry, if only in the movies. Someone is in trouble and needs a doctor to save their life. However, there is a cry of another kind in Isaiah. And that cry is a proclamation of the holy Lord. Isaiah 6:1 says, "I saw the Lord sitting on a throne, high and lifted up, and the train of His robe filled the temple."

The glory of the Lord is incredible and unparalleled! It is phenomenal! God's holiness resounds. His holiness expands Heaven and earth. Nothing compares. Nothing even comes close. His grandeur fills the temple. Revelation 15:3-4 extols the magnificent and holy Lord. "They sing the song of Moses, the servant of God, and the song of the Lamb, saying: 'Great and marvelous are Your works, Lord God Almighty! Just and true are Your ways, O King of the saints! Who shall not fear You, O Lord, and glorify Your name? For You alone are holy. For all nations shall come and worship before You, for Your judgments have been manifested.'"

Psalm 24:10 says, "Who is this King of glory? The Lord of hosts, He *is* the King of glory. *Selah.*" Psalm 97:9 tells us, "For You, Lord, *are* most high above all the earth; You are exalted far above all gods." Psalm 99:3 exclaims, "Let them praise Your great and awesome name—He *is* holy." A holy God reigns from Heaven and spans the universe.

THOUGHT FOR THE DAY
God is holy, and there is none like Him.

PRAYER
Lord, let everything that has breath praise You—on the rooftop and in the valley. Praise the holy God Who is and was and is to come. Praise the Lord. In Jesus' name, Amen.

Your Sins Are Forgiven

"When Jesus saw their faith, He said to the paralytic, 'Son, your sins are forgiven you'" (Mark 2:5).

READ: MARK 2:1-5

A lovely little violet grew along the stony path to the lake. A passerby walked to the lake one sunny day. Stumbling, he stepped on the little purple flower and crushed it. But the flower releases a delightful scent into the air. It exchanged its life for the gift of fragrant perfume.

When Jesus died on the cross, He released forgiveness to humanity in exchange for His life. All God requires is that we receive His forgiveness by repenting of our sins and wrongdoing and believing in Jesus as our Savior. Jesus sets us free from past sins and promises life eternal when we believe in Him. This gift of forgiveness exceeds any wrongdoing we have committed. No sin is too great for God to forgive when we ask. Only believe.

THOUGHT FOR THE DAY
When I place my faith in Him, God exchanges my sin for His forgiveness.

PRAYER
Lord, I exchange my careless days without a thought of You for a new life filled with hope and joy the moment I choose You. In Jesus' name, amen.

Rest, Refresh, and Reboot

"Then Jews from Antioch and Iconium came there; and having persuaded the multitudes, they stoned Paul and dragged him out of the city, supposing him to be dead" (Acts 14:19).

READ: ACTS 14:19-22

Some heavy use of the computer tired not only the programmer but also the computer. The computer locked up and froze, refusing to function after its over-extended use. The only solution was to shut it down and let it reboot. The off switch proved a handy button that allowed it to refresh and regenerate.

Sometimes, we are like the computer. We need to refresh and reboot after intense trials and temptations. Burdened down with the cares of life, we can overextend our usefulness or burn out in serving the Lord. Galatians 6:9 encourages us, "Let us not grow weary while doing good, for in due season we shall reap if we do not lose heart."

We need a season of rest to refresh ourselves. Paul was once stoned, dragged outside the city, and left for dead. But God renewed his life. He wasn't dead, after all. All he needed was the touch of God's hand, which caused him to spring back to a life of service. God pushed the refresh button for Paul, and he charged ahead. He got his second wind and proclaimed the Gospel of Christ to those who gave him up for dead.

During our season of rest and refreshing, we must stay connected to the Lord. Unlike the computer, we must not turn off the switch that connects us to God. Instead, we need a direct current flowing through the Holy Spirit to our inner person. Prayer provides that continuous flow of the Holy Spirit to our innermost being.

As we step out of our old patterns, we can regenerate our dedication and service to God. A refreshing change in ministry, a new approach to serving God, or even a pause in pursuing success in the secular world may provide a breath of much-needed revival for our spirits.

God awaits us in this season of rest and renewal. Let us continue to place Him first as we journey through life.

THOUGHT FOR THE DAY

Just as in a car, computer, or other things, I need to pause, refresh, and regenerate.

PRAYER

Thank You, Lord, for waiting on me, helping me, and guiding me through every station of life. I place my life in Your loving hands in times of rest and service. In Jesus' name, amen.

Focused on God's Goodness

"In this manner, therefore, pray: Our Father in heaven, Hallowed be Your name. Your kingdom come. Your will be done On earth as it is in heaven. Give us this day our daily bread. And forgive us our debts, As we forgive our debtors. And do not lead us into temptation, But deliver us from the evil one. For Yours is the kingdom and the power and the glory forever. Amen" (Matt. 6:9-13).

READ: MATTHEW 6:5-13

The crowd shouted triumphantly as all eyes focused on the winning pass that scored the touchdown. Another win for the home team.

As we focus on the goodness of God, we realize His mercy and love extend beyond anything we might imagine. We can look around and see the magnificent beauty of His creation. The golden sunset, the ruby-throated hummingbird, the majestic mountains, the radiant rose, and the sparkling stars all display the grand Artist at work. His creation resounds with beauty and grace.

Even if we closed our eyes, the work of the Artist remains. We can witness the grandeur of the Creator when we hear the rushing waterfall, the buzzing bees, and the babbling brook. The soft raindrops, the sun's warmth, and the refreshing breeze come from the Lord. God is the ultimate Creator of a vast universe which speaks of His glory, and His design is glorious.

God is good to give us such beauty to fill our earth. But reaching beyond the mere physical, God is good in other significant ways. His mercy and love fill our lives. That mercy for sinful people springs forth from His love for His creation. The evidence of God's mercy and love is the sacrifice of His only begotten Son, Jesus. Jesus died so that we might live. He took our place on the cross. Unless Christ returns, we will all experience death. But we are offered eternal life by believing in Jesus as our Savior. God grants eternal life to anyone who accepts Jesus into their hearts. All we must do is believe.

THOUGHT FOR THE DAY
God reveals His goodness in a spectacular and awesome display throughout our universe. His power and glory rule over creation.

PRAYER
Heavenly Father, help me focus on Your goodness, glory, power, mercy, and love.
In Jesus' name, amen.

Don't Go It Alone

"But the Helper, the Holy Spirit, whom the Father will send in My name, He will teach you all things, and bring to your remembrance all things that I said to you" (John 14:26).

JOHN 14:26-28

To the lost hiker, the wilderness seemed to ramble on forever. He referred to the survival guide he brought until he could manage his way out of the woods. He quickly used the guide's advice for finding water: gather dew overnight by tying a plastic bag to a tree limb. The guide also counseled him to mark his path so that he did not go in circles. Since there was no one else to turn to, he relied on his skills and the survival guide.

We may feel all alone in life's journey. We may feel as if we are going in circles. All seems lost. We may have experienced betrayal, unemployment, an accident, disease, a failed promotion, abandonment by a child or parent, or divorce. The Holy Spirit awaits us, desiring to guide and comfort us. He urges us to turn to Him. Psalm 145:18 says, "The Lord *is* near to all who call upon Him, To all who call upon Him in truth."

Jesus asked, "My God, My God, why have You forsaken Me" (Mark 15:34). Because He asked that question, we don't need to. God has not forsaken us; He is only a prayer away. When Jesus asked that question, He cried out with a loud voice. We may cry out to God with a loud voice or whisper a prayer in our thoughts. However we approach the Lord, we can know God's Spirit will comfort and guide us. "Draw near to God and He will draw near to you" (James 4:8).

THOUGHT FOR THE DAY

When all seems lost, and there's no one to turn to, the Spirit supplies my heartfelt needs to comfort and guide me.

PRAYER

Lord, continually remind me of Your presence in my life. May the Spirit always be with me—leading, guiding, and comforting me. In Jesus' name, amen.

What Wondrous Love

"He who does not love does not know God, for God is love" (1 John 4:8).

READ: 1 JOHN 4:7-12

Turning to Polly the parrot, Patrick the parrot proclaimed, "I love you." Polly replied, "Prove it."

Words accompanied by appropriate actions offer proof. This is true even when it comes to love. To say we love someone holds greater significance and believability when we do something to prove it. Actions substantiate our words. Kind and loving actions prove we love other people.

God proved His love for humanity when Jesus went to the cross. "In this the love of God was manifested toward us, that God has sent His only begotten Son into the world, that we might live through Him" (1 John 4:9).

God does not merely give lip service to proclaim His love for us. Instead, He sent His only begotten Son to die so that we would not have to die. Jesus died for us while we were yet sinners. The cross testified to God's love when Jesus gave His all so we might realize His best. He offers us His best when we accept His sacrifice. The blood of Jesus Christ sets us free. His best not only awaits us in eternity but also provides for us now. Our life devoted to doing God's will ensures an optimum journey to our heavenly home.

THOUGHT FOR THE DAY
What wondrous love God has for us, not only in eternity but also for now.

PRAYER
Heavenly Father, thank You for preparing for me the best possible life on earth and eternity.
In Jesus' name, amen.

Treasures

"Every good gift and every perfect gift is from above, and comes down from the Father of lights, with whom is no variation or shadow of turning" (James 1:17).

READ: JAMES 1:2-18

The sound of birds singing, the smell of bacon frying, the soft mist of raindrops upon our skin, and the beauty of a golden sunset all speak of God's treasures. The Creator God surrounds us with life's wonderful and beautiful treasures that are nothing short of spectacular.

Maybe we drive only the best car, live in the biggest house, and wear the most expensive labels. Perhaps, vast and lavish luxuries surround us. Yet there are far greater treasures than these. God provides for joy, love, and peace when we commit our life to Him. His mercy and kindness extend great treasures to us. The fruits of the Spirit are God's gifts: love, joy, peace, long-suffering, gentleness, goodness, faith, meekness, and temperance. Focusing upon Him and doing His will ensures we will experience the goodness of God in the most unexpected ways.

As we focus upon God's beauty and surplus in our lives and commit ourselves to Him totally, His abundant riches unfold in ways we can only imagine.

With a commitment to God, we will never fail to live in the best He has for us. A life lived for the Lord produces results far beyond the treasures this world might offer. As it says in 1 John 2:25, "And this is the promise that He has promised us—eternal life."

THOUGHT FOR THE DAY

Treasures are not only those we see and touch. The fruits of the Spirit—such as love, joy, and peace—supply us with riches, too.

PRAYER

Lord, thank You for the treasures of life You so bountifully give me. In Jesus' name, amen.

Exploring the Bible

"Be diligent to present yourself approved to God, a worker who does not need to be ashamed, rightly dividing the word of truth" (2 Tim. 2:15).

READ 2 TIMOTHY 2:14-16

Geologists collect data to analyze and evaluate the most likely location of gold deposits on the earth. They often dig long trenches to determine if core drilling is beneficial. This process allows them to calculate the quantity and value of the gold and other metals in the ground. The purpose of exploration is to locate desirable deposits of gold that are economical to mine.

Likewise, believers are inclined to explore the Bible for gold nuggets of truth that are vital to our spiritual well-being. Furthermore, the true disciple of Christ mines deeply for the truths of God. We read Scripture, then study and meditate on that Scripture so that we glean wisdom and guidance from the principles.

Proverbs 2:1-5 instructs us to receive the words of God and treasure His commands as we would seek for silver or hidden treasures. Then, we will understand the fear of the Lord and find God's knowledge. Seeking God through deeply exploring and studying the Bible accomplishes much in our spiritual life. Meditating on God's Word provides a more profound discovery of His doctrine, increased knowledge of His commands, a richer belief in His principles, and a greater understanding of His will. Exploring God's truths and considering His ways equip us to live a faithful life.

THOUGHT FOR THE DAY
God expresses His truths throughout Scripture.

PRAYER
Lord, give me a desire to live for You, know Your will, and apply it to my life as You reveal it to me through the Bible. In Jesus' name, amen.

Helmet of Salvation

"And take the helmet of salvation, and the sword of the Spirit, which is the word of God" (Eph. 6:17).

READ: EPHESIANS 6:11-19

Known as the home of the Kentucky Derby, Churchill Downs Racetrack conducts thoroughbred horse racing in Louisville, Kentucky. Several traditions also play a significant role in the Derby atmosphere. Revelers show up in the infield to party with unbridled restraint. "Millionaire's Row"—the expensive box seats—attract the rich and the famous. Women wear elegant outfits, lavishly accessorized with large, elaborate hats. The rich and famous show off their fancy hats in quite a show that competes with the traditional Easter bonnet sported by many churchgoers on Easter Sunday. Someone jokingly said, "A hat covers a multitude of sins."

Another type of protective head covering is used in football games. Players use helmets to protect their heads from injury. Players complete their outfits with shoulder pads, cleats, and knee pads. After all, this is a rough and challenging game where protection is vital to the player.

Ephesians tells of another type of head covering that is spiritual—the helmet of salvation. God's power allows everyone who believes through faith in the redemptive work of Jesus Christ upon the cross to find salvation (Rom. 1). Acts 4:12 says, "Nor is there salvation in any other, for there is no other name under heaven given among men by which we must be saved." Without the helmet of salvation, we are vulnerable and unprotected against our enemy. Hebrews 2:3 asks, "How shall we escape if we neglect so great a salvation, which at the first began to be spoken by the Lord and was confirmed to us by those who heard *Him?*" The helmet of salvation protects us from the enemy of our soul. Let us suit up with this indispensable piece of armor.

THOUGHT FOR THE DAY
The whole armor of God surrounds and encompasses the believer who is ready to win the battle for the Lord. The helmet of salvation is the most essential tool the believer has.

PRAYER
Lord, protect me spiritually with the helmet of salvation as I go forth in my daily living.
In Jesus' name, amen.

Waiting and Waiting

"In these lay a great multitude of sick people, blind, lame, paralyzed, waiting for the moving of the water" (John 5:3).

READ: JOHN 5:2-9

Waiting is not easy. After years of waiting after becoming paralyzed by a stroke, my grandmother lay in bed. She spent her remaining time waiting for the passing of days. Unable to speak, she repeated, "Vaiting, vaiting, and vaiting," which we understood to mean "waiting, waiting, and waiting." She smiled and laughed whenever my young son visited. She teased him as he walked to her bedside with a milk bottle dangling from his mouth, and she pretended to keep it. She had a playful spirit amid suffering.

Grandmother led a fruitful and productive life. She grew a large vegetable garden, canned her produce, and shared it with her neighbors. A skilled seamstress, she sewed clothes for her family and made quilts from the scraps. She was a real winner in the game of life, laughing and loving to the end. But for those who knew her, life on the couch was a sad end to a productive life. She waited for healing that never came.

Some have watched desperately as loved ones have left this life, never receiving healing. Maybe a mother's baby was taken prematurely, or an accident claimed a young father's life. Such profound loss is hard to reckon. We're not exempt from human suffering.

Christ suffered the ultimate sacrifice. Even God experienced tragedy as He watched the death of His Son on the cross. The utmost hope is expressed in Matthew 16:25: "For whoever desires to save his life will lose it, but whoever loses his life for My sake will find it."

THOUGHT FOR THE DAY
Waiting on the Lord, I will put my trust in Him.

PRAYER
God, make me a person accepting of Your divine plan even when I don't understand. In Jesus' name, amen.

Persist in Prayer

"Pray without ceasing" (1 Thess. 5:17).

READ: 1 THESSALONIANS 5:15-22

Praying sustains us. Whether praying for our needs, others' needs, or thanking God, prayer sustains us. In the same way, a continued prayer life maintains us, keeping us on course. We can continue our spiritual journey through sincere and devout prayer. It connects us to God and feeds our souls. Without prayer, we sever the link with our Creator.

This is why Scripture instructs us to pray without ceasing. Prayer is the conduit through which our communication with God flows—our direct current to Him. Praying to our Heavenly Father joins our hearts to His. We cannot have a personal relationship with the Lord without prayer. Prayer is our open line of communication with a loving Father.

Prayer does not have to be formal—with folded hands and bended knees—to be effective. Someone once said, "My best prayer was prayed when I was hanging onto the end of a rope dangling forty feet from the top of a building." This was a heartfelt prayer.

Prayer that reaches the portals of Heaven comes from a deep, genuine need to express our thoughts to the Lord. Prayer keeps us in rhythm with God's will and is fundamental to a successful spiritual life where God is the key focus. Commit your ways to Him as you pray without ceasing.

THOUGHT FOR THE DAY
God is just a prayer away.

PRAYER
Lord, I don't want my prayer to be just a beep on the radar of my spiritual life. I want to make prayer resound and dominate my life so that I may be closer to You. In Jesus' name, amen.

Treasures of the Palace

"I will take you as My people, and I will be your God. Then you shall know that I am the Lord your God who brings you out from under the burdens of the Egyptians" (Exod. 6:7).

READ: EXODUS 6:5-8

Dazzling! A castle sitting atop a mountain in the Ozarks displays the opulence reserved only for the wealthy. The gold-gilded treasures in the castles of Europe demonstrate the riches of royalty. Excess and abundance dominate the art and architecture of the rich and famous.

Most of us will never live in a palace or a castle, but believers who continue in the faith have a trove of treasures awaiting them on the other side. "But as it is written: 'Eye has not seen, nor ear heard, nor have entered into the heart of man the things which God has prepared for those who love Him'" (1 Cor. 2:9).

Scripture reveals some of the treasures the Lord has in store for us when we leave this earth and enter His glory. Of course, it's only a partial description of the beauty of Heaven, but we understand from Revelation 22:1-2 that a pure river of life, as clear as crystal, flows from the throne of God. In the middle of its street and on either side of the river, the tree of life stands and yields fruit for the healing of the nations.

A glimpse into this glory shows us a great city, the holy Jerusalem, descending out of Heaven from God with a glorious light, like a most precious gem. The city is pure gold, like transparent glass. Precious stones—such as sapphire, emerald, topaz, and amethyst—adorn the foundations of the city's wall. A view of the city's twelve gates reveals gates of pearl and a street of pure gold. The glory of God illuminates the city, and the Lamb of God is its light (Rev. 21-22).

There will be a new Heaven and a new earth. "And I heard a loud voice from heaven saying, 'Behold, the tabernacle of God *is* with men, and He will dwell with them, and they shall be His people. God Himself will be with them *and be* their God. And God will wipe away every tear from their eyes; there shall be no more death, nor sorrow, nor crying. There shall be no more pain, for the former things have passed away'" (Rev. 21:3-4).

THOUGHT FOR THE DAY

Believers have the promise of a home in Heaven with our Father that transcends anything on earth.

PRAYER

Heavenly Father, I long for that city where You await me. My new home is reserved for me when I place my hope in You. It is phenomenal because You designed it but, most of all, because You reside there with us. Your presence makes it perfect. In Jesus' name, amen.

Do You Need Comfort?

"Blessed are *those who mourn, for they shall be comforted" (Matt. 5:4).*

READ: MATTHEW 5:2-4

A three-year-old boy cried uncontrollably when his dad failed to catch a ball tossed into the stands at a Texas Rangers game. Missing the ball was more than the little tyke could handle. Unbridled emotion erupted as he missed getting the souvenir ball. But a happy ending followed. When a Ranger in the dugout saw what had happened, he tossed the little boy's daddy a ball. Thrilled with his catch, the child now sleeps with the baseball, comforted with his prized Texas Rangers souvenir.

When life has dealt us pain and penalties and we can't bear the burden ourselves, we can remember a loving and merciful God stands in the shadows to heal our hurts and deliver us. When we're not happy with the way our lives are going, we can find comfort by leaning on the Lord. Time heals a hurting heart when God comforts us. He promises to comfort us when we cling to Him.

As you wait on the Lord, let Him heal the grief with the comfort only He can bring. That still, small Voice from Heaven consoles our broken hearts and soothes our pain.

THOUGHT FOR THE DAY
When we are suffering from the trials of life, God waits in the shadows to comfort us.

PRAYER
Lord, I pray for your comfort when all else fails me. You are "my rock and my salvation" (Psalm 62:2), a real presence amid my sorrow. Thank You. In Jesus' name, amen.

You Are Infinitely Valuable

"And all flesh shall see the salvation of God" (Luke 3:6).

READ: LUKE 3:4-6

During the Covid pandemic, doctors, nurses, and medical personnel—as well as food workers and others—were considered essential employees. Others were considered expendable and lost their jobs. Tragic consequences followed. The devastation of the disease encompassed many with sorrow, loss, pain, and grief.

But God deems everyone essential. We are born into this world because of God's love. God has a Divine design for each of us. He yearns for us to accept Jesus Christ as our Savior so we can spend eternity with Him in Heaven. And He equips us with the means to do just that.

John 3:16 says, "For God so loved the world that He gave His only begotten Son, that whoever believes in Him shall not perish, but have everlasting life." There are no exclusions. We who desire to spend eternity with our Heavenly Father need only accept Jesus Christ. Once we do, He fully forgives us.

Once forgiven, our identity changes. God forgives us for every wrongdoing—past, present, and future. We don't have to struggle to receive God's acceptance. We will desire to please the One Who created us. Should we fail—and we will—all God requires is that we confess our sin, turn from our wicked ways, and seek His face. God is ready to receive and forgive us instantly, completely, and eternally. We can't earn our salvation. All we must do is believe.

God awaits us with outstretched hands and an open heart because He values us. We are all essential to God.

THOUGHT FOR THE DAY
You are essential. God created you to be loved by Him. He loves you simply because He created you.

PRAYER
Lord, thank You for the gift of life and the hope of eternal life with You. Thank You for considering each of us essential to Your kingdom. In Jesus' name, amen.

Divinely Warned

"So, the Lord said, 'I will destroy man whom I have created from the face of the earth, both man and beast, creeping thing and birds of the air, for I am sorry that I have made them'" (Gen. 6:7).

READ: GENESIS 6:5-8

A young man careened down the highway on his motorcycle, enjoying the warm sunshine and beautiful scenery. He sped along with the wind in his face, making time as the lines in the meridian flashed by. Suddenly, something—or Someone—told him to slow down. He listened since he was in unknown territory. He soon came to an intersection. Crossing his path was a sizeable one-ton truck that would have leveled him had he been cruising at his previous speed. However, a Divine source unknown to him had warned him, sparing his life.

Divine warnings alert us in ways we can't understand. God tells us to slow down on a spiritual level, turn from our wicked ways, and repent. He wants us to change direction and implement a moral compass that points to godly behavior.

This moral compass is the Bible, along with the direction of the Holy Spirit. As 2 Timothy 3:16-17 says, "All scripture *is* given by inspiration of God, and *is* profitable for doctrine, for reproof, for correction, for instruction in righteousness, that the man of God may be complete, thoroughly equipped for every good work."

Grasp every bit of the Bible as if it were the last thread on which you must hang. Make it your lifeline. Your soul depends on it. And if God is warning you of impending danger, turn to Jesus as your Source and Strength. Repent and get right with God.

THOUGHT FOR THE DAY
Our moral compass is the Bible. When we make a wrong move, God warns us.

PRAYER
Lord, when I make a terrible choice, make me aware. As You warn me of my wrong directions and bad decisions, help me turn from my wicked ways and repent. Help me to cling to You and be faithful to Your Word. In Jesus' name, amen.

Got Jesus?

"For God so loved the world that He gave His only begotten Son, that whoever believes in Him should not perish but have everlasting life" (John 3:16).

READ: JOHN 3:16-17

Flipping through a magazine, we might find an advertisement with an actor sporting a white mustache. Along with the picture are the words, "Got milk?" We might counter with a more substantial question: "Got Jesus?" Those who realize the impact of that question know Jesus is the One Who delivers us from sin and offers eternal life. John 3:17 says, "For God did not send His Son into the world to condemn the world, but that the world through Him might be saved." And Jesus said of Himself in John 14:9, "He who has seen Me has seen the Father." Jesus fulfilled God's will by offering Himself as a sacrifice for our sins. God makes us His child through the new birth. Through Jesus' substitution, we can become children of God.

Some may want the product (promise) without the process (commitment). When we commit our lives to Christ, He promises us an eternity where we will share the streets of gold and drink from the river of life. Revelation 21:3, 7 says, "And I heard a loud voice from heaven saying, 'Behold, the tabernacle of God *is* with men, and He will dwell with them, and they shall be His people. God Himself will be with them *and be* their God . . . He who overcomes shall inherit all things, and I will be his God and he shall be My son." Because of God's grace, we are the children of God.

Without God's forgiveness, we would all be lost. Since Jesus took our place and died on the cross in our place, we can experience the fullness of God; but our merit has nothing to do with this position. Jesus' redeeming death on the cross does. His resurrection is the spiritual bridge between God and us.

When Adam and Eve sinned in the Garden of Eden, God could have turned his back on them. But because of His love, He provided a means for redemption. A God of mercy saw our value. In His infinite love, He reached down, stretched out His arms of love, and rescued us.

THOUGHT FOR THE DAY

We are rescued, delivered from our sinful past, and brought into communion with God by His mercy. He claims us as His own. Jesus' blood covers our shame. We are children of the King.

PRAYER

Lord, I thank You I am Your child because of what Christ did on the cross. In Jesus' name, amen.

Everything We Need and Then Some

"And God is able to make all grace abound toward you, that you, always having all sufficiency in all things, may have an abundance for every good work" (2 Cor. 9:8).

READ: 2 CORINTHIANS 9:6-15

Realizing the need for shoes, clothing, and toiletries for the people in Africa, a generous donor offered a bountiful supply of these. Exceeding expectations, a shoe manufacturer donated three large appliance boxes full of new shoes for children in Africa. Other businesses supplied necessities such as soap and shampoo. Shipping containers overflowed. More freight containers had to be procured to provide adequate storage for the shipment. What an excellent problem to encounter. God's blessings on this project were overwhelming.

God instructs us to give liberally from the abundance of our hearts. The person who sows sparingly will reap sparingly. But those who sow bountifully will reap bountifully. God loves a cheerful giver. We should give lavishly, not grudgingly. As God enriches us with material things, we can help supply the needs of others. We glorify God with liberal giving. As we increase our giving, God increases the fruits of our righteousness. We will have everything we need, and then some.

THOUGHT FOR THE DAY
You can't outgive God.

PRAYER
Thank You, Lord, for Your gifts to me. Thank You for Your Son, Jesus. Thank You, too, that because of Him, I have eternal life. In Jesus' name, amen.

Who Has the Last Word

"I am the Alpha and the Omega, the *Beginning and* the *End, the First and the Last" (Revelation 22:13).*

READ: REVELATION 22:12-13

"Is so!"

"Is not!"

"Is so!"

"Is not!"

"Is!"

"Ain't!"

The young boys argued back and forth, each wanting to prove he was right. It was the last straw in a stubborn match. Who won the argument? Who would have the last word?

God wants us to relinquish our right to be heard, our right to be first, our right to be correct, and our right to have the last word. When we give up our dictates, we position ourselves where God can use us. When we think more of others than ourselves, we live out James 4:10: "Humble yourselves in the sight of the Lord, and He will lift you up."

When we put God first, we position ourselves for a win-win situation. We gain God's approval, love, and mercy. And we prove ourselves to be His loyal servant. God doesn't want us to be wise in our opinion or self-will. He wants us to submit to His will. Romans 12:1-2 says, "I beseech you therefore, brethren, by the mercies of God, that you present your bodies a living sacrifice, holy, acceptable to God, *which is* your reasonable service. And do not be conformed to this world, but be transformed by the renewing of your mind, that you may prove what *is* that good and acceptable and perfect will of God."

THOUGHT FOR THE DAY

A prayer of surrender means I give up my will for God's will in my thinking, prayers, desires, dreams, and actions—never demanding of God but denying my preferences and pleasures for God's ways and His will.

PRAYER

Lord, help me relinquish my dreams and desires as I surrender to You. Your sufficiency is more than enough. Your grace grants the gifts of completion, perfection, and mercies. My goal is to please, honor, serve, obey, and love You. When I abandon my will and accept Your will, I glorify You. In Jesus' name, amen.

Getting Rid of Bitterness

"Let all bitterness, wrath, anger, clamor, and evil speaking be put away from you, with all malice" (Eph. 4:31).

READ: EPHESIANS 4:31-32

Have you ever seen a disgrace that you respond to lividly? Maybe someone placed a box of chicken bones in the parking space next to the one you pulled into at the mall. Perhaps someone sped recklessly around you on a dangerous curve, or maybe someone sprayed graffiti on a church. A person misbehaves, possibly breaking the law. Such situations can make our blood boil. We want to get even with the miscreant. We want justice. It only seems fair that the offender deserves punishment equal to the crime.

In like manner, we have all offended God. None of us are perfect. The Bible tells us God is just, so we wonder why God doesn't get even. We sometimes ask this question about others, but we overlook our wrongdoing and pretend we are above the law. If God were to get even with every offender, no one would go unpunished. Romans 3:23 says, "All have sinned and fall short of the glory of God." *All* means no exceptions. Only Jesus was perfect. We can't tag other people's failings as sins while excusing ours as mistakes or slip-ups.

Anytime we fail to meet God's standards, we fail God. However, we are not to throw our hands up and resign ourselves to sin. Although we can never achieve perfection, we should turn to God and ask for forgiveness when we fail. Romans 5:1 promises, "Therefore, having been justified by faith, we have peace with God through our Lord Jesus Christ." Once we ask God for forgiveness, we must turn from our wicked ways and commit ourselves to move forward toward godly behavior with the help of the Holy Spirit.

THOUGHT FOR THE DAY
We are saved by grace because of Jesus' death on the cross and His resurrection from the dead.

PRAYER
Lord, give mercy and grace. Though I deserve none, please forgive me. In Jesus' name, amen.

No Doubt About It

"But let him ask in faith, with no doubting, for he who doubts is like a wave of the sea driven and tossed by the wind" (James 1:6).

READ: JAMES 1:5-8

A kite that sails in the clear blue yonder will toss about with the wind if not anchored or controlled. Once it is high enough, we can release the guide string, and the kite will take off like a frenzied, half-crazed goose. The kite is driven and tossed by the tempestuous wind when set free from its anchor, flitting about until it finally crashes.

Likewise, a believer who is not anchored to a solid foundation of faith in God is driven and tossed by every doctrine or idea. Doubt assails them like a stormy sea—a spiritual tsunami of sorts.

What is the cure for doubt? Are we doomed to wander in doubt and confusion? No, we have a solution for our questions and doubts. We can benefit from the story of a father who sought help from Jesus for his son who suffered convulsions. "Jesus said to him, 'If you can believe, all things are possible to him who believes.' Immediately the father of the child cried out and said with tears, 'Lord, I believe; help my unbelief'" (Mark 9:23-24).

At times, questioning, considering, or even doubting is not unusual. Unsolved puzzles and unanswered questions fill our lives. We are no less Christian when we ponder the possibilities, conjecture the outcome, or debate the choices. A strong, sound analysis considers the facts and proves we are utilizing our God-given mental skills.

Our unbelief leaves when we turn our doubt to God and ask for His help. He never fails to help those who ask.

THOUGHT FOR THE DAY
When doubts arise, my anchor is fastened to the Rock of Ages.

PRAYER
Lord, I believe. Please help me when unbelief assaults my faith. In Jesus' name, amen.

Easy to Forgive

"And forgive us our debts, As we forgive our debtors" (Matt. 6:12).

READ: MATTHEW 6:9-15

A carpenter in the building trade knows the value of a saw with a diamond blade. Diamond blades are generally not used for cutting wood but are preferred for cutting stone, concrete, asphalt, bricks, glass, and ceramics. Additionally, they are used for cutting semiconductor materials in the IT industry and for cutting gemstones in the gem industry. Diamonds cover some cell phone protectors, and some ultra-rich drive cars embellished from fender to fender with genuine diamonds.

In Jeremiah 17:1, the prophet describes a peculiarly unique pen with a diamond point: "The sin of Judah *is* written with a pen of iron; With the point of a diamond *it is* engraved On the tablet of their heart, And on the horns of your altars." A diamond blade can cut straight lines in tile and masonry, but steel blades are better for wood. The material to be cut determines the best blade to use.

A parallel application in the spiritual world involves our tendency to use a harsher standard when forgiving ourselves. At times, the most difficult person to forgive is ourselves. The Bible says love covers a multitude of sins. We need to forgive ourselves since we, too, are God's children and worthy of His love, mercy, and forgiveness. Jesus says, "This is My commandment, that you love one another as I have loved you" (John 15:12). We are worthy of being loved because of the One Who created us. Therefore, we are worthy of forgiveness—from others and ourselves.

THOUGHT FOR THE DAY
Have mercy on yourself because you are God's creation for whom Christ died.

PRAYER
Lord, when I beat myself up for the wrongs I have done, remind me that You died for me and count me worthy. Your love, mercy, and forgiveness are applied when I ask for it as I forsake my wrongdoing and turn to spiritual righteousness found only in You. When I find forgiving myself difficult, remind me that Christ's atonement paves the way for me to forgive myself. In Jesus' name, amen.

A Healthy Diet

But He answered and said, "It is written, 'Man shall not live by bread alone, but by every word that proceeds out of the mouth of God'" (Matt. 3:4).

READ: MATTHEW 4:3-4

I enjoyed lunch with a friend. We watched what we ate and cut back on sweets and high-calorie foods. After finishing our sandwiches, the waitress asked if we would like to have a free slice of chocolate cake. We both smiled but declined the offer. Moments later, the waitress passed by our table with a small portion of cake someone hadn't finished. We eyed the cake. Stopping the waitress, my friend asked if she would please bring her a piece of cake. The temptation wasn't as strong until we saw the cake. The tempting thing for me was it was free. But I also knew free didn't apply to calories. I sat abjectly as my friend enjoyed her cake. I asked if she liked it. She answered, "It was okay, but I shouldn't have eaten it."

Sin is like the cake. Although it looks good from a distance, it provides a heartbreaking disappointment. God knows this and tries to prevent our hurt by instructing us to live a pure life by obeying the guidelines in His Word. He does not ask us to live a pleasureless life, but He wants His children to experience happiness and peace of mind.

With the help of the Holy Spirit, we can live consistently with the teachings of God's Word. Doing so will please us and bring joy.

Do you need to go on a spiritual diet, cutting out the sinful fat of your carnal nature? Has sin tipped your spiritual scales? Our physical bodies perform best when we make wise choices about food, and we thrive spiritually when we feast on God's Word. We find joy by living a holy life.

THOUGHT FOR THE DAY
When I sacrifice my passions and adopt God's will, I place God at the center. Then I will surrender my will to God's, making it possible for the Holy Spirit to reign in my life.

PRAYER
Lord, help me to watch and pray so that I avoid temptation. "The spirit indeed is willing, but the flesh is weak" (Matt. 26:41). In Jesus' name, amen.

Be Brave in Doing God's Will

"The king loved Esther more than all the other women, and she obtained grace and favor in his sight more than all the virgins; so he set the royal crown upon her head and made her queen instead of Vashti" (Esther 2:17).

READ: ESTHER 2:17-20

Today, the winners of beauty pageants receive armloads of red roses, sparkling crowns, exotic trips, and extravagant gifts. But the beauty contest winner in the Old Testament book of Esther saved an entire nation.

King Ahasuerus sat on the throne, displaying his kingdom's riches and His Majesty's splendor. He commanded Queen Vashti's presence, wanting to parade her beauty for all to see. When Queen Vashti refused to obey the king's order, he was furious. He gathered all the beautiful young virgins for a beauty contest, planning to replace Queen Vashti. Among the beauties was Esther, a ravishing Jewish orphan raised by her uncle, Mordecai. Esther obtained favor from all who saw her. The king chose her as the new queen.

Once queen, Esther continued to obey the commands of her uncle, who instructed her to keep her heritage a secret. Queen Esther intervened when the king gave a decree to destroy all the Jews. She and all the Jews fasted. Bravely, she declared, "If I perish, I perish" (Esther 4:16).

Esther was also wise. One way to a man's heart is through his stomach, so she prepared a feast for the king—not once, but twice. After dining, the king granted her requests. Her bravery, beauty, and wisdom saved the Jewish people. But more so did her surrender to God.

THOUGHT FOR THE DAY
Wisdom is necessary to do God's will, as is bravery.

PRAYER
*Lord, help me find favor in Your sight. Guide me with wisdom and strength.
In Jesus' name, amen.*

Nothing Is Too Big for God

"When Jesus heard it, He said to them, 'Those who are well have no need of a physician, but those who are sick. I did not come to call the righteous, but sinners, to repentance'" (Mark 2:17).

READ: MARK 2:3-17

Imagine receiving a diagnosis for an incurable illness. Knowing your days are numbered, you decide to celebrate the last weeks of your life by taking an exotic vacation to Europe. Soaking up the good life, you dine at the best restaurants, tour the most lavish castles and museums, and purchase the most luxurious items. You decide to return home after weeks of extravagant living. However, after a visit to the clinic, you learn your life has taken a dramatic and positive turn. You were misdiagnosed. Your health is not endangered, nor are your days numbered. You are released from your prison of hopelessness. New life pours through your veins. You have a new lease on life.

The paralytic was ecstatic when his friends lowered him from the roof of the house into the midst of the crowd where Jesus stood. He expected Divine healing. After all, Jesus was known far and wide for His healing ministry. But what may have surprised him was Jesus' words: "Son, your sins are forgiven you" (Mark 2:5). His spiritual failures rivaled the disease in his body. Yet Jesus saw his spiritual and physical needs and addressed them both. Jesus proved there was no need beyond His reach.

Jesus still does this. When we allow Him to reign over our body, mind, and soul, He proves willing and able to meet our needs. Nothing is beyond His reach; no need is too great. He is the Almighty God, the Alpha and Omega, the Messiah. He created us and can heal us. He is the great I Am, and all things are under Him.

THOUGHT FOR THE DAY
My small thinking does not limit God.

PRAYER
Heavenly Father, remind me You are willing and able to meet all my needs, both small and large, when I allow You into my life. May I never shut You out of any area of my life but open wide my arms of acceptance to Your Divine will. In Jesus' name, amen.

Our Battles Belong to the Lord

"The Lord will fight for you, and you shall hold your peace" (Exod. 14:14).

READ: EXODUS 14:13-18

Some struggle to earn good grades. I was one of them. As a youngster in junior high, I took a course in typing. Although I had calculated my final grade to be an A, the teacher awarded me a B. I turned to my friend who sat behind me, and we compared our grades. Disappointed, I showed him my final score was lower than I had expected. He understood and then approached the teacher, pleading with her to change my grade to an A. She agreed. My friend won the battle for me with his reasoning and power of persuasion. All I had to do was watch the discussion from a distance and smile when the teacher nodded her approval to his request.

We face many spiritual battles that entail many threatening situations and struggles. We fight for our rights, employment, marriages, and children. We jockey for greater independence, increased income, better health, or more friends. Sometimes after we resolve one battle, two others face us. However, the Lord fights our battles when we allow Him. Then, when we move out of the way, God paves the way for success in all life's situations and provides for all our needs.

Our responsibility is to hold our peace and let Him perform His will in all areas of life. When we cease struggling for an answer and rest in God's presence, His peace will surround us, giving us power, protection, and provision.

THOUGHT FOR THE DAY
The battle belongs to the Lord.

PRAYER
Heavenly Father, help me to rest in Your provision. May Your peace fill me with assurance as I commit my battles to You. In Jesus' name, amen.

Transformed from the Inside Out

"And do not be conformed to this world, but be transformed by the renewing of your mind, that you may prove what is that good and acceptable and perfect will of God" (Rom. 12:2).

READ: ROMANS 12:1-2

Reality television transforms everything from cars to houses to people. A couple leaves their average-looking house to return shortly and find a jewel of a home, radiating beauty beyond their wildest imagination. Workers have knocked out walls, raised ceilings, and stripped floors—sometimes, they have eliminated entire rooms. Although the owners may have lived in the residence for years, they may not even recognize it.

Turning to another program, we may be awed by an impoverished person whose appearance is altered to a near-celebrity level of a stunning beauty equal to a Hollywood star—complete with regal attire and dazzling jewelry. Some cars are even changed into virtual hotels with hot tubs in the back seat.

These transformations utilize existing elements—only the outward appearance is changed by adding and subtracting where necessary. First Corinthians 15:51-52 reveals a spiritual change: "Behold, I tell you a mystery: We shall not all sleep, but we shall all be changed—in a moment, in the twinkling of an eye, at the last trumpet. For the trumpet will sound, and the dead will be raised incorruptible, and we shall be changed."

But how do we get from point A to B, where God changes us from mortal to immortal? Jesus explains how this transformation takes place: "Most assuredly, I say to you, unless one is born of water and the Spirit, he cannot enter the kingdom of God. That which is born of the flesh is flesh, and that which is born of the Spirit is spirit" (John 3:5-6). And again, "For God so loved the world that He gave His only begotten Son, that whoever believes in Him should not perish but have everlasting life. For God did not send His Son into the world to condemn the world, but that the world through Him might be saved" (John 3:16-17). We experience the power of God to transform when we believe in His Son, Jesus Christ.

THOUGHT FOR THE DAY
We are transformed from mortal to immortal through belief in God's Son.

PRAYER
Lord, renew, change, and transform me into Your image so I might please You. In Jesus' name, amen.

Make This Your Season

"I said in my heart, 'God shall judge the righteous and the wicked, For there is a time for every purpose and for every work'" (Eccl. 3:17).

READ: ECCLESIASTES 3:17-18

Super Bowl 2012 was a fantastic game between two incredibly talented teams: the New York Giants and the New England Patriots. The New York Giants won a hard-fought battle and defeated the New England Patriots by a narrow margin of 21-17. With only fifty-seven seconds left in the game, the Giants scored a six-yard touchdown to win the Super Bowl title. Both teams played hard during the regular season to compete in the NFL championship. The Giants' victory proved the team's skill and determination.

Perhaps, you are celebrating some victories of your own in this season of your life. Things are going well, and life is on the upswing. A job promotion, a new home, a new baby, or many things have brought you success. Life is sweet. You feel joy and are savoring victory.

Or maybe you are experiencing a downward spiral. Things just aren't going your way. Perhaps you lost your job, have a loved one who has strayed from God, or are facing a downward spiral in your health. You may feel as if your life is spinning out of control. You ask, "When will it ever end?"

We may not understand why things are the way they are, but we can be confident God is there for us. He is forging the path ahead. When we accept that we are not in control, we can let go, let God, and experience victory. We cannot correct things by scheming or trickery. When we submit to God's will, He will make this the season where we realize His love, but we must be patient as we allow Him to work out these things. The answer will come when we seek, pray, and wait on God.

Whether you are on an uphill journey or a downhill slide, let Jesus be the Lord of your life. Whatever season you are in, let the Lord permeate it with His love as you surrender to that love.

THOUGHT FOR THE DAY
In season and out, in victory or defeat, the Lord loves and cares for us.

PRAYER
Lord, reign in my life in whatever season I am. Your love surrounds me wherever I might be. I owe You my all. In Jesus' name, amen.

What Scares Me Most

"If we confess our sins, He is faithful and just to forgive us our sins and to cleanse us from all unrighteousness" (1 John 1:9).

READ: 1 JOHN 1:8-10

What scares me the most is the devilish thing I might do next. Will I smart off and say something I regret? Will I cut someone off in traffic? Will I push someone in the buffet line, or will I hang up on someone on the phone? Or worse yet, will I kick the dog, throw the cat, or deliberately splash mud on a passerby? I am sure the wrong decision will come sooner or later. It's just a matter of when.

First John 1:8 says, "If we say that we have no sin, we deceive ourselves, and the truth is not in us." Why try to kid myself? Often, temptation comes daily. The question is whether I will overcome or be drawn into the temptation and fail the test.

Jesus Christ is the only Person Who has walked the earth yet never sinned. But, of course, doing so wasn't easy for Him, either. After forty days of fasting in the wilderness, the tempter came to Him with greater temptations than we have ever encountered. The devil encouraged Jesus to turn stones into bread, which must have seemed like a feast fit for a king after forty days. After all, Jesus was human as well as God. But Jesus passed the test with flying colors. The devil continued tempting Jesus with other tests, but Jesus passed those, too. Throughout His life on earth, Jesus proved Himself over and over.

I'm not on the same spiritual level as Jesus and have failed numerous times. One definition of sin is "missing the mark." But we have an Advocate with our Heavenly Father through Jesus (1 John 2:1). When we turn from sin, repent, and ask for forgiveness, "[Jesus] is faithful and just to forgive us *our* sins" (1 John 1:9). Although I miss the mark, I am assured of total forgiveness when I turn to God. Because of Jesus, we have hope.

THOUGHT FOR THE DAY
Fearing no more failures, I can turn to God and find mercy and grace when I repent.

PRAYER
"Heavenly Father, I depend on You to forgive me when I repent and trust in the blood of Jesus to cover my sins. In Jesus' name, amen.

Deed to a Fishing Pole

"Nevertheless, lest we offend them, go to the sea, cast in a hook,
and take the fish that comes up first.
And when you have opened its mouth,
you will find a piece of money;
take that and give it to them for Me and you" (Matt. 17:27).

READ: MATTHEW 17:24-27

As young boys, my husband and his brother, Don, enjoyed summer days hunting, fishing, playing, and enjoying carefree days on their grandparents' farm. They would climb trees, explore the woods, and tease the bulls in the pasture. Corn-cob fights broke out when their cousins came to visit. It was harmless fun—the kind of fun boys enjoy.

Catfish filled the pond on the farm. Don enjoyed fishing in the pond so much that he asked his grandma if she would give it to him. So, she wrote a title deed to the pond on a scrap piece of wood with Don's name as the property owner. Then, she staked it into the ground. When the farm was sold years later, Don fondly remembered owning a piece of his grandparents' land with the pond. He cherished the memories he had as a young boy. The family shared many good meals from the fish caught from that little pond.

Not only did Jesus provide food from the seas for His disciples, but He also shared tax money. Today, He provides eternal life to those who believe—just as He called the four fishermen to be His disciples, so He calls us to take up our cross daily and follow Him.

THOUGHT FOR THE DAY
Jesus provided then, and He provides now.

PRAYER
Lord, help me never to forget You are my Source. Thank You for meeting my physical and spiritual needs. In Jesus' name, amen.

The Promise of Power, Peace, and Purpose

"In Him you also trusted, after you heard the word of truth, the gospel of your salvation; in whom also, having believed, you were sealed with the Holy Spirit of promise" (Eph. 1:13).

READ: EPHESIANS 1:13-15

Someone once said, "My wife can go from zero to 160 in a second." When someone asked how, the person responded, "When she gets on the scales at home."

The power of a car engine is measured in horsepower, which determines how fast a car can go. Power measures how fast energy is produced.

John says, "But as many as received Him, to them He gave the right to become children of God, to those who believe in His name: who were born, not of blood, nor of the will of the flesh, nor of the will of man, but of God" (John 1:12-13). Now, that is power—true power, mighty power, unsurpassed power—power for the taking simply because we accept Jesus Christ as Savior. This promise delivers ultimate power beyond explanation and the promise of an eternal relationship with our Heavenly Father.

But we don't have to wait for eternity to receive God's promises. The promise of peace accompanies the promise of power. Jesus says, "Peace I leave with you, my peace I give to you: not as the world gives do I give to you. Let not your heart be troubled, neither let it be afraid" (John 14:27). Although the world might rage, the peace of God can reign in our hearts when we cling tightly to Him—trusting in Christ to sustain us, see us through, and deliver us through the storms of life.

The most incredible peace comes from serving God's purpose. We do His purpose best when we are in the center of His will by glorifying Him in all our ways, serving Him in our actions, and trusting Him in whatever situations we encounter. Jesus tells us to love God with our hearts, souls, and minds (Matt. 22:37). That is our purpose on earth.

THOUGHT FOR THE DAY
Power, peace, and purpose are fulfilled in the believer who places God first in everything they think, say, and do.

PRAYER
Lord, help me depend on You and Your promises as I journey through life. In Jesus' name, amen.

How Much Sin Is Too Much?

"For all have sinned and fall short of the glory of God" (Rom. 3:23).

READ: ROMANS 3:23-26

A thief escaped the clutches of the law after robbing a bank of thousands of dollars. His crime defied human law and God's commandment in Exodus 20:15: "You shall not steal." The act also violated morality and was a sin.

On the other hand, two couples were playing a card game. The men went outside for a break between games, and one of the ladies said, "Let's stack the deck so we can win. They won't know the difference, and it won't matter. It's such a little thing."

Bank robbery is a recognizable sin in common law and God's eyes. But could such a little thing as cheating at a game of cards possibly be considered a sin? Yes. Even such a small wrong displays dishonesty. Although the men may never have known about the deceptive act, God would know. God cannot tolerate dishonesty.

We might ask, "How much sin is too much sin?" Any sin is too much sin. Maybe we haven't robbed a bank or cheated at a card game, but we can think of other ways we have failed God, ourselves, or others. Perhaps we have maligned another person's reputation with rumors or misrepresented the truth on a job application. Maybe we cheated on a test, read a dirty book, or exaggerated our expense account. Perhaps we looked at obscene pictures on the internet, on a cell phone, or in a movie. John says, "If we say that we have no sin, we deceive ourselves, and the truth is not in us" (1 John 1:8).

However, God provides a remedy. John also says, "If we confess our sins, He is faithful and just to forgive us our sins and to cleanse us from all unrighteousness" (1 John 1:9). We must not continue sinning but, instead, turn to God and depend upon Him to provide an avenue of escape. We will never be perfect or exempt from sin, but when we fail, "we have an Advocate with the Father, Jesus Christ the righteous" (1 John 2:1).

THOUGHT FOR THE DAY
Sin is inevitable, but God will cure us when we confess our sins to Him.

PRAYER
Lord, I'm not perfect and never will be. Remind me You forgive me if I confess my sins in true repentance. And when I do fail, remind me Jesus is my Advocate. In Jesus' name, amen.

What Will Be Your First Words?

"And every creature which is in heaven and on the earth and under the earth and such as are in the sea, and all that are in them, I heard saying; 'Blessing and honor and glory and power Be to Him who sits on the throne, And to the Lamb, forever and ever'" (Rev. 5:13).

READ: REVELATION 5:11-14

What do you think you will say at your first sight of God upon entering Heaven? Will it be "Wow," "Thank You," "How did I ever make it," or "Are You for real?" Maybe you will pinch yourself and blink your eyes quickly several times in amazement—stuttering in wonder and unable to utter anything coherent. God's Word says every creature will say at least one thing. We will worship by proclaiming, "Blessing and honor and glory and power to Him who sits on the throne and to the Lamb, forever and ever!"

All of God's creation acknowledges and proclaims His brilliant and excellent glory with praise. This proclamation is a personal and sincere declaration of the power and grandeur of God Almighty—not just a corporate chant. No silent prayers embarrassingly whispered so no one can hear. Instead, we will all exclaim the goodness of God and of the Lamb Who sits on the throne. Everyone and everything will declare God's majesty.

THOUGHT FOR THE DAY
Lord, I worship You today. The fullness of Your glory has not yet been seen or heard but will on that glorious day when we see You face to face in eternity.

PRAYER
Thank You, Lord God Almighty, for creating me as a part of Your universe. I give You glory and honor now but enthusiastically await the day when I will see You face to face and count myself among all Your creation who gives You the praise You deserve. In Jesus' name, amen.

Punch List

"And if I go and prepare a place for you, I will come again and receive you to Myself; that where I am, there you may be also" (John 14:3).

READ: JOHN 14:1-4

Larry, a homebuilder, was completing the construction of a large house. The homeowners were excited to move in and set up their furnishings, so they met with Larry and made an extensive list of items that needed attention for finalization. They listed even the most minute details—a punch list. Finalization lay a couple of weeks out, but Larry attended to every detail one by one. Moving out of the old house and into the new one would soon be a reality for the couple. But first, they had to discard useless items they had accumulated so they could make room for the new.

We, too, will one day move from our earthly house to our heavenly home. Doing so will be a wonderful and grand occasion. Preparing for this joyous move entails a spiritual punch list. The top of our list should include making God our priority. Other things on the list should be expressing love; being faithful in prayer, Bible study, tithing, and worship; forgiving others who have wronged us; and abstaining from harmful habits while replacing them with good habits. Practicing godliness and purity assures us we will be ready when God calls us home.

THOUGHT FOR THE DAY
My real home is where Jesus is.

PRAYER
Prepare me, Lord, for eternity. Thank You for my heavenly home. In Jesus' name, amen.

Hurts, Habits, and Hang-ups

"But God demonstrates His own love toward us, in that while we were still sinners, Christ died for us" (Rom. 5:8).

READ: ROMANS 5:6-15

Drug and alcohol habits are habits that destroy. But they are not the only hang-ups that cross the line. Cursing, gluttony, pornography, lying, and stealing are destructive habits, too. Some sear their consciences when maligning sins catch them. A growing footprint of sinful habits and hang-ups is often not tamed for those who immerse themselves in evil. Sin attracts the spiritually unconscionable. The results are pain and sorrow that hurt them and others. Sin immerses us in pain, anguish, and grief.

Thankfully, many seek a lifestyle of good morals by attuning themselves to biblical principles. Shifting our focus from sinful behavior to faith and purity is not a mystery but a method. The core of our being depends on the godly principles proclaimed in the Bible and sensitivity to the Spirit's nudging. The Bible's spiritual food gives us the strength to overcome bad behavior and sinful habits. The Spirit is the still, small voice Who prods us to make good decisions and convicts us when we don't. Our choices are influenced by the Spirit when we quiet ourselves and listen to His voice.

THOUGHT FOR THE DAY
Hurts, habits, and hang-ups propel the immoral to live outside God's will, but the Spirit draws us to a righteous life that pleases God.

PRAYER
Lord, help me close the gap on sin and open my eyes, ears, and heart to Your Word as the Holy Spirit draws me to You. In Jesus' name, amen.

Out of the Shadows

"Every good gift and every perfect gift is from above, and comes down from the Father of lights, with whom there is no variation or shadow of turning" (James 1:17).

READ: JAMES 1:13-17

Saying "hello" to a pair of brown shoes on the front porch is not my typical greeting. However, it was still somewhat dark outside when I placed the mail in the box. I mistakenly assumed the shoes were a little, brown, speckled alley cat that had been hanging around. But when I looked more closely, I saw it was not Happy, our adopted cat, but my husband's muddy shoes. The shadows concealed the identity.

Shadows can conceal, making things appear as something else. The darkness of night conceals some sins. A burglar intending to plunder a home often waits until the cover of night. Clandestine relationships may occur in the shadows of the dark, too.

But our Heavenly Father shines a light on our deeds with His all-knowing eye. He is the Father of lights, shining His beauty, truth, and glory on all.

When we accept the grace and mercy of the Lord, we step out of the darkness and into the light where He awaits us. He is holy and righteous, and His presence has no darkness or shadows.

THOUGHT FOR THE DAY
God's goodness, mercy, and love outshine the sun.

PRAYER
Lord, let me not be guilty of hiding from Your presence, but may I ever seek Your face and tender hand of mercy and grace. In Jesus' name, amen.

Awaken Me

"And the Lord called Samuel again the third time. So he arose and went to Eli, and said, 'Here I am, for you did call me.' Then Eli perceived that the Lord had called the boy" (1 Sam. 3:8).

READ: 1 SAMUEL 3:2-10

When children play "Red Rover," they shout to the team on the opposite side, "Red Rover, Red Rover, let Johnnie come over." The person whose name was called races to break the human chain that the other team's linking hands have formed. If they break the chain, that team claims one of the other players for their side. If they fail to break the chain, the person goes to the opposing team. The game continues until all the team players have been called. The team with the most players at the end of the game wins.

Young Samuel heard God's call three times. He mistakenly thought it was Eli who had called him. Eli denied calling the boy and told him it was God calling Samuel. The word of the Lord was rare in those days, so this was a unique experience. Samuel answered the call of God after listening intently for the message.

We, too, must listen for God's call. We respond when we turn away from things that distract, listen for God's call, and answer with a ready reply that proves our willingness. We may not hear God's voice audibly, but we can hear the soft voice of the Holy Spirit drawing us to Him. Like Samuel, we should be eager to hear God's Word, however rare it might be. As we learn to listen, God will open our hearts to more of His bidding.

THOUGHT FOR THE DAY
God's call is only a breath away.

PRAYER
Lord, open my ears to listen to You and my heart to do Your bidding. In Jesus' name, amen.

Beautiful You

"He has made everything beautiful in its time. Also He has put eternity in their hearts, except that no one can find out the work that God does from beginning to end" (Eccl. 3:11).

READ: ECCLESIASTES 3:11-15

Some children enjoy paint-by-number art kits. The kits require almost no talent or skill, yet a pretty and colorful picture emerges when the paintings are completed. They make instant artists out of ordinary people. Rembrandt would be proud.

While the painting progresses, it may look more like a jumbled-up mess with no order or plan—a mass of lines and numbers and blocks of space mingled with no apparent design. But a beautiful painting materializes if they are executed according to the instructions. The painting is a visual masterpiece of sorts.

Just as it takes time and effort to complete the painting, so does progress in our spiritual life. To achieve our spiritual calling, we must open our hearts to God. Once we have accepted Christ, we must continue to submit to the wooing of the Holy Spirit so He can complete His work in us. Only when we concede to God's will are we spiritually complete. True beauty comes from knowing the Lord and living for Him.

Just as God has made everything beautiful in its time, so we are a work in progress. He makes order out of our otherwise chaotic life. He connects the dots and colors in the spaces to form a spiritual life filled with order and purpose. As we invest our lives in doing His will and give Him reign, God creates a complete painting with design and purpose.

THOUGHT FOR THE DAY
True beauty comes from knowing and serving God.

PRAYER
Lord, help me to recognize Your Divine will and plan. I realize a beautiful life when I place You in the center of everything I do. In Jesus' name, amen.

Just Because

"By faith Sara herself also received strength to conceive seed, and she bore a child when she was past the age, because she judged Him faithful who had promised" (Heb. 11:11).

READ: HEBREWS 11:1-11

Young children often question when they don't understand. Likewise, adults often answer that question with "just because." Children learn the reasoning behind the premise, while adults avoid explanation for many reasons. At times, adults have merely exhausted their ability to explain. The conclusions to a barrage of questions may end with a simple, "Just because."

In Hebrews 11, we learn Sara bore a child because she acknowledged God's faithfulness to His promise. She is a heroine of faith in God. Counted as a star among believers, she never doubted God's commitment to His word. Even at an old age, Sara embraced God's promises as infallible, undeniable truth. Even in her old age, Sara never gave up. Hope prevailed—simply because God said it.

THOUGHT FOR THE DAY
God said it; I believe it; and it's done.

PRAYER
God, please give me the faith of a mustard seed to believe. Your word never fails, and we trust You to stand true to the promises You give. In Jesus' name, amen.

Think of a Word

"For God so loved the world that He gave His only begotten Son, that whoever believes in Him should not perish but have everlasting life" (John 3:16).

READ: JOHN 3:16-17

What would you say if someone asked you to think of a word that best describes your feelings about God's saving grace? If you can't think of only one, try two or more that describes how you feel about what God has done for humanity and you personally. My short list would be grateful, overwhelmed, and undeserved. But, of course, I could think of more: relieved, ecstatic, hopeful, triumphant.

John 3:16 tells us how God expressed His love. He made it so simple to receive His gift of salvation that all we must do is believe—not pay with money, work with your hands until they are raw, think through complex math problems or grammatical dissections of sentences, live in a beautiful house, drive a fancy car, or wear designer clothes. All God requires is belief. John 1:12 says, "But as many as received Him, to them He gave the right to become children of God, to those who believe in His name."

THOUGHT FOR THE DAY
Believing is receiving.

PRAYER
Lord, I thank You for Your gift of salvation, which I cherish. When I feel inadequate or unworthy, remind me Your gift saves me. In Jesus' name, amen.

Our Long-Awaited Wedding Day

"Go forth, O daughters of Zion, And see King Solomon with the crown With which his mother crowned him On the day of his wedding, The day of the gladness of his heart" (Song of Songs 3:11).

READ: SONG OF SOLOMON 3:6–11

Some children's stories tell of a brave knight who can win the maiden's hand in marriage if only he can kill the fire-breathing dragon. I recall only one accurate account that tells how the strong, majestic, and godly groom wins the bride by experiencing his death. The union is future-tense in a time and place accompanied by a grand marriage supper—the marriage supper of the King of kings and Lord of lords with His bride, all believers. This union was accomplished but not yet realized when Jesus gave His life on the cross. Those who acknowledge and accept the redemptive act of salvation are promised an eternal home with their Savior.

The spiritual marriage between Christ and His Church resounds with the love of God for His people.

THOUGHT FOR THE DAY
As days come and go, we are one day closer to our eternal home with the One Who loves us and gave His life for us.

PRAYER
Heavenly Father, thank You for the hope of Heaven and our union with Jesus, Who saves us from all sin and care. In Jesus' name, amen.

Present Tense

"For I consider that the sufferings of this present time are not worthy to be compared with the glory which shall be revealed in us" (Rom. 8:18).

READ: ROMANS 8:18–39

As he struck out, the little leaguer announced, "Someday, I'm going to be a World Series winner!" After failing a physics course, the college student said, "Someday, I'm going to be a renowned physicist." After rejection from numerous publishers, the author proclaimed, "Someday, I will appear on the *New York Times* bestseller list." All these accounts look to a future victory.

While not wrong to take our defeats and determine to do better, many of us live outside the present. Rather than living in the moment, we look to the future as if it were a fairytale or dream. Some riddle their lives with worry over future events that never happen, while others reminisce over the past. Savoring a long-ago victory—or remorseful over past defeats—some ignore present opportunities. As a result, we deny today's reality and refuse to take up our cross and follow God daily.

We should live life to the fullest and seek to be all God wants us to be in this moment because the present is all we have. Serving God with all He has given us and using our time wisely are the keys for a well-lived life. We must live in the reality of today with God at the helm. We should not be reluctant to seek excellence in all we do because God deserves the best from us in the time we are given.

THOUGHT FOR THE DAY
Yesterday is only a memory, and tomorrow may never be.

PRAYER
Lord, remind me that each day is a treasure. Let me live that day as if it were my last by honoring and serving You. In Jesus' name, amen.

Fully Surrendered to God

"So he answered and said, 'You shall love the Lord your God with all your heart, with all your soul, with all your strength, and with all your mind,' and 'your neighbor as yourself'" (Luke 10:27).

READ: LUKE 10:25-28

During my college years, I was required to take a course in business statistics for my marketing major. As a non-linear thinker, I struggled to tackle the course. I had already had to take remedial math. I remember the professor saying, "Don't do this half-heartedly. It requires all your effort." I passed the course, but not without complete resolve, intense study, and hard work.

God wants us to love Him with our hearts, souls, minds, and strength. Our goal should be a full-strength dedication to God. We must give one hundred percent to please the Lord—nothing barred. If we try to skim by with as little as possible, we won't grow spiritually or reach our goal of complete dedication. The Christian faith requires full throttle ahead.

To love the Lord with all your heart requires sincere dedication; to love the Lord with all your soul requires a focused determination; to love the Lord with all your strength requires daily application, and to love the Lord with all your mind requires a scriptural foundation.

As we live for Him, we must target all areas of our lives as outlined in Luke 10.

THOUGHT FOR THE DAY
Total devotion to God means a full work-out of all my senses, surrendering all.

PRAYER
Heavenly Father, I give my life to You in complete surrender. Help me apply biblical principles to my life as I live for You. In Jesus' name, amen.

Do You Have a Warranty?

"Nevertheless, the solid foundation of God stands, having this seal: 'The Lord knows those who are His,' and 'Let everyone who names the name of Christ depart from iniquity'" (2 Tim. 2:19).

READ: 2 TIMOTHY 2:19-22

Dreams are strange things sometimes. While putting on his shoes in his dream, my husband once asked, "Do my tennis shoes have a warranty?" Although comical and out of sorts with reality, the dream caused me to reflect. What would a warranty on tennis shoes look like? Would it cover running fast, jumping radically, getting the shoes wet, or leaving the shoes in the sun over an extended time?

I then pondered the ramifications of a spiritual warranty. Do we need a guarantee from God concerning our salvation—a seal of approval, perhaps? According to the Bible, we are sealed with the Holy Spirit. Ephesians 4:30 tells us not to "grieve the Holy Spirit of God, by whom you were sealed for the day of redemption." When we believe, God sends the Holy Spirit to live in us until the day of our final redemption, when God will take us home and change us into His glorious image.

Walking in the Spirit requires time in God's Word and sensitivity to His voice. Paul writes, "We are bound to give thanks to God always for you, brethren beloved by the Lord, because God from the beginning chose you for salvation through sanctification by the Spirit and belief in the truth" (2 Thess. 2:13). The Spirit draws us to Christ, and once there, He seals us. This is God's guarantee—a warranty until He changes us from glory to glory.

THOUGHT FOR THE DAY
The Holy Spirit puts His seal of approval upon me when I accept Jesus as my Savior.

PRAYER
Lord, keep me close to You until the day of my redemption when I return home to You.
In Jesus' name, amen.

Puddle-busters

"And such were some of you. But you were washed, but you were sanctified, but you were justified in the name of the Lord Jesus and by the Spirit of our God" (1 Cor. 6:11).

READ: 1 CORINTHIANS 6:9-20

For some five-year-olds, puddle-jumping might be viewed as a sport—as pole-vaulting is for a more mature athlete. But my young son found greater joy in jumping in the mud puddle than in jumping over it. Likewise, splashing in the shallow pools of rainwater in our front drive brought laughter.

My husband built a sandbox from brick in the backyard and filled it with a large load of sand. The sand satisfied our son—for a while. He and his friends made mountains and dug tunnels, but the fascination faded. Not satisfied with sifting the sand through his fingers and slipping it through his toes, our son desired more solid dirt. I watched as they drug the water hose to the sandbox and buried themselves in wet, sandy mud. Their jeans changed from blue to a muddy brown, as if they had been dyed. I stopped the water overflow but not before it had done its damage. Our washing machine got a good workout.

We all have dirtied our lives with sin. Deep in it, we need help to get cleaned up, and God does just what we need. He sent Jesus to cleanse us from sin, washing us whiter than snow. When we turn our lives over to Him, He salvages our souls.

THOUGHT FOR THE DAY
God trades our rags for robes of white when we turn our lives over to Him.

PRAYER
Thank You, Lord, for giving me a new life in Christ. Help me to shun all appearances of evil. When I do wrong, forgive me and set me on the right path again. In Jesus' name, amen.

Commit Yourself to Action

"For as the body without the spirit is dead, so faith without works is dead also" (James 2:26).

READ: JAMES 2:24-26

The race was a stampede at break-neck speed. The runners charged toward the end goal, and the winner was announced. In his victory speech, the champion declared that his drive to win pushed him harder as he neared the finish line. He was motivated to succeed.

What is all-encompassing for you? What drives you with a passion? What is the wind beneath your wings? Maybe a better question would be, "Who is the wind beneath your wings?" Is it your mate, parents, child, or boss? Who motivates you to be productive? Does your ego drive your motivation to out-perform? Or does an outside force—others or God—motivate you?

If God is our Motivator, we have chosen wisely. Galatians 6:8-9 says, "For he who sows to his flesh will of the flesh reap corruption, but he who sows to the Spirit will of the Spirit reap everlasting life. And let us not grow weary while doing good, for in due season we shall reap if we do not lose heart." God offers everlasting life through faith in Jesus Christ. Guiding and drawing us to Christ, the Spirit nudges us toward Jesus Christ, Who died for us.

This move toward Christ propels us to love Him, seek Him, serve Him, turn from our wicked ways, and draw near to Him. When we accept Jesus, we desire to commit to action, promote the kingdom, and live godly lives. The fruit of the Spirit is love, joy, peace, longsuffering, kindness, goodness, faithfulness, gentleness, and self-control. Paul says in Galatians 6:10, "Therefore, as we have opportunity, let us do good to all, especially to those who are of the household of faith." Our love for God motivates us to serve others, and the fruit of the Spirit manifests itself in action.

THOUGHT FOR THE DAY
Motivation garnered through the Holy Spirit results in godly application and action.

PRAYER
Lord, move me to action. Never allow me to be mediocre. Give me opportunities to help others and to glorify You. In Jesus' name, amen.

Never Look Back

"Brethren, I do not count myself to have apprehended; but one thing I do, forgetting those things which are behind and reaching forward to those things which are ahead" (Phil. 3:13).

READ: PHILIPPIANS 3:12-14

Looking in my clothes closet, I reminisced over the clothes I could wear when I was younger and slimmer. My form was better, and so was my general physical fitness. Trying on clothes at the dress shop was easier on my psyche. However, that was over thirty years ago. Age and time define what I am today.

Looking in life's rearview mirror, we may recall happy or regretful moments. Life is tangled with a vast array of experiences, good and bad. God admonishes us to forget those things behind us and focus on what we can accomplish for Christ now.

Longing for what was prevents us from living for Jesus in the present. We bog down in our spiritual life. Paul exhorts us to move forward: "I press toward the goal for the prize of the upward call of God in Christ Jesus" (Phil. 3:14).

We need to impact our world and others now. Life is too full of possibilities to let them pass because we envision a different personal history. Our past has involved both positive and negative, but we shouldn't live there. Where necessary, we should ask for the Lord's forgiveness. Then, we need to move on, living for today as if it is the last day of our lives.

THOUGHT FOR THE DAY
Both good and bad are a part of life. Living for God today is what matters most.

PRAYER
Lord, when I forget Your goodness and long for days gone by, remind me I have a calling to press toward the goal for the prize You promise. In Jesus' name, amen.

Consequences

"Then Joseph's master took him and put him into the prison, a place where the king's prisoners were confined. And he was there in the prison" (Gen. 39:20).

READ: GENESIS 39:6-23

A popular game show called *Truth or Consequences* once aired on television. The contestants received roughly two seconds to answer a trivia question before the buzzer sounded. If the contestant answered the question incorrectly, consequences followed—usually a lighthearted or giddy stunt. Bob Barker hosted the show from 1956 to 1975 and announced at the end of each episode, "Hoping all your consequences are happy ones."

We know from experience that consequences are not always pleasant. Perhaps we gave a flippant answer that caused hurt feelings, cut someone off in traffic, or made a wrong movie choice. Your bad decisions or foul actions could have even resulted in tragic consequences.

In contrast, you may have made the right choice and stood firm for godly principles. You did what was right and yet experienced an unforeseen loss. Joseph did this. When Potiphar's wife tempted him with her charm, he resisted and ran from the temptation. But he still stood in harm's way. Angry and wanting revenge, she falsely accused him, which resulted in his imprisonment. Joseph's righteousness resulted in punishment rather than reward. Even so, he stood firm in his commitment to God. He was the winner because he was unyielding in his faith.

THOUGHT FOR THE DAY
We are never guaranteed a reward for our good behavior. Nevertheless, we must strive to make godly choices.

PRAYER
Lord, regardless of my actions' consequences, help me do what is right. In Jesus' name, amen.

Quit Beating Yourself Up

"Or do you not know that your body is the temple of the Holy Spirit who is in you, whom you have from God, and you are not your own? For you were bought at a price; therefore glorify God in your body and in your spirit, which are God's" (1 Cor. 6:19-20).

READ: I CORINTHIANS 6:17-20

Some young ladies once discussed the school's homecoming queen, saying she had a sweet spirit as well as being pretty. After the game, at the victory party, the girls chatted and asked what the girl's secret was, She told them she didn't deserve the title. She was just an ordinary girl who got lucky.

A far cry from this is the person who toots their own horn. With a superior attitude, that person claims to know it all, to look down on others, and to champion their own cause. Such people have a condescending attitude that appalls others rather than appeals.

Others constantly belittle themselves and criticize everything they do. They beat themselves up for not saying the right thing, saying too much, not saying enough, wearing the wrong clothes, living on the wrong side of town, or not measuring up.

This type of degradation is not biblical. God has made us in His image, and our bodies are the temple of His Spirit. God loves and cherishes us so much that He sent His Son to die for our sins. Since God made us in His image, we should realize our self-worth. God does not create junk. We are children of the king.

THOUGHT FOR THE DAY
Though I might discredit my value, God sees me for what I am and still loves me.
Therefore, I esteem myself worthy of being called His child.

PRAYER
Dear Lord, help me realize my worth in You. In Jesus' name, amen.

Imitators of Christ

"Brethren, join in following my example, and note those who so walk, as you have us for a pattern" (Phil. 3:17).

READ: PHILIPPIANS 3:13-21

The seamstress carefully laid out the pattern on the beautiful silk fabric. Royalty would wear the evening gown. The seamstress must measure everything accurately along the lines of the paper pattern for the most flattering fit. If she executed her task exactly, the dress would enhance the beauty of the fabric and the one who wore it.

Our pattern to follow is the example of Christ. We must conform to His standard. Jesus displayed the righteousness of God by submission to the Father. He moved in the power of the Holy Spirit. Jesus exemplified holy living by preaching the kingdom of God and teaching a Gospel that honored God. He healed and performed miracles. We should pray for God's strength so that we can do God's work.

Just as Jesus was baptized in water, so we, too, should display our faith through the same. Acts 10:48 says, "And he commanded them to be baptized in the name of the Lord." We must not remain silent about our faith but should glorify God by teaching others so that they may believe, too. We can also imitate Jesus by praying for healing and Divine intervention for the needy. John wrote, "Beloved, do not imitate what is evil, but what is good. He who does good is of God, but he who does evil has not seen God" (3 John 1:11).

We should pattern our life after Jesus. Acts 11:16 says, "Then I remembered the word of the Lord, how He said, 'John indeed baptized with water, but you shall be baptized with the Holy Spirit.'" In John 3:5, Jesus said, "Most assuredly, I say to you, unless one is born of water and the Spirit, he cannot enter the kingdom of God."

We should imitate Jesus as He imitated His Heavenly Father. The Bible says, "Then Jesus answered and said to them, 'Most assuredly, I say to you, the Son can do nothing of Himself, but what He sees the Father do; for whatever He does, the Son also does in like manner'" (John 5:19).

THOUGHT FOR THE DAY
I please the Heavenly Father when I mirror the image of Christ.

PRAYER
Lord, help me be more like You each day. In Jesus' name, amen.

Prayer as a Priority

"Then He spoke a parable to them, that men always ought to pray and not lose heart" (Luke 18:1).

READ: LUKE 18:1-8

"Chicken Little" is a children's fairytale that dates to the early nineteenth century. Chicken Little is a chick who believes the sky is falling when an acorn falls on its head. The little chicken panics and then goes on a journey to tell the king. The story is of despair as the little chicken imagines the tragic consequences of the sky falling by continually repeating, "The sky is falling!"

Some of us mimic Chicken Little. We imagine the worst possible scenarios. We spend our time worrying and fretting over things that are only real in our imaginations. Often, our worst apprehensions never materialize, yet we fear and dread fills our minds. What a load of relief we could experience if we would only turn our problems over to the Lord. Instead of spending countless hours worrying, we should first go to God in prayer.

Whether real or imagined, we should address our problems to the Lord. He is a loving and caring God. He wants to shoulder our burdens; prayer allows Him to work on our behalf. As we turn our problems over to Him, we will find He is able and willing to meet our needs.

Make prayer your priority. Allow God to work. Send Him the message that you need help by falling on your knees and asking Him to intercede in your problems, real or imagined.

THOUGHT FOR THE DAY
Praying first for God's help makes everything that comes afterward more accessible to His will.

PRAYER
Lord, let me lift my voice to You, knowing Your Divine plan is the perfect plan.
In Jesus' name, amen.

God's Delay Isn't God's Denial

"But the angel said to him, 'Do not be afraid, Zacharias, for your prayer is heard; and your wife Elizabeth will bear you a son, and you shall call his name John'" (Luke 1:13).

READ: LUKE 1:5-14

What do you do while you wait? You may listen to the radio at a stoplight or count how long it takes for the light to change. You may view the magazines at the grocery store or pick up some candy as you wait in the checkout line. You may visit the hospital with family or even pray for those hurting. You may get fidgety and restless as you wait your turn in whatever situation. You may even get cranky and throw things.

How many of us do as Elizabeth and her husband, Zacharias, did as they waited for a child? Zacharias was a priest. Elizabeth was barren and elderly, but she dreamed of someday being a mother. Despite her condition, she and her husband did not live a life of dissipation or neglect God's commands. Nor were they bitter toward God. They followed God's commands, including the one that said not to covet what others have and to remain pure. They were blameless. What a great testimony.

At times, they may have grown weary, watching and waiting for God to give them the desire of their hearts. But they never wavered from their faith or wandered from righteous living. God delayed their immediate gratification, but God did not deny them. Instead, God provided a son that would herald the way of the Savior, Jesus Christ. This son was unique in the timing and evidence of his godliness—the Spirit filled him while still in his mother's womb. John readied a people who waited for the Messiah.

THOUGHT FOR THE DAY

What do I do with my time while waiting for God to answer my prayer? Do I patiently look forward with joy to His answer, or do I become bitter and angry while I wait? God may answer my prayer with a yes, a maybe, a later, or a no. I must patiently wait until He delivers an answer.

PRAYER

Lord, help me live righteously until You show me what You want in my life, whether I receive my expected outcome or not. May Your will be done. In Jesus' name, amen.

Where Are We Headed?

"For our citizenship is in heaven, from which we also eagerly wait for the Savior, the Lord Jesus Christ" (Phil. 3:20).

READ: PHILIPPIANS 3:18-21

Going places? Maybe to the beach, the mountains, or the zoo? Whatever your vacation destination, many plan to enjoy the time spent away from their daily routine. Often, vacation travel equips us to be happier and more relaxed. New experiences, increased enjoyment, and greater life satisfaction spring from vacation time when we leave the boring behind us. We are usually less stressed, more energetic, and more enthused. When traveling, our happy place consists of living each day as if it were the first day of our honeymoon. However, vacations are temporary. We spend most of our lives doing the ordinary. Anticipating the next most exciting event might bring momentary happiness, but life continues as we live it.

To gain momentum and satisfaction as we move toward our goals requires focusing on what matters most: eternity. After all, our stint on earth is short. Then, we move to our eternal future. Who, what, when, where, and how questions equip us to prepare for that eternal destination. Who provides the means to a heavenly future? Jesus Christ died for our sins so that we might have eternal life (John 3:14-15.). What awaits us? Revelation 21:3 says, "And I heard a loud voice from heaven saying, 'Behold, the tabernacle of God *is* with men, and He will dwell with them, and they shall be His people. God Himself will be with them *and be* their God.'" When does this happen? Jesus said, "And behold, I am coming quickly, and My reward *is* with Me, to give to everyone according to his work" (Rev. 22:12). Where? Revelation 21:1-2 says, "Now I saw a new heaven and a new earth, for the first heaven and the first earth had passed away. Also, there was no more sea. Then I, John, saw the holy city, New Jerusalem, coming down out of heaven from God, prepared as a bride adorned for her husband." Finally, how does one reach their eternal home? Romans 10:9 says, "That if you confess with your mouth the Lord Jesus and believe in your heart that God has raised Him from the dead, you will be saved."

THOUGHT FOR THE DAY

Romans 6:23 promises us that "the gift of God is eternal life in Christ Jesus our Lord."

PRAYER

Lord, prepare me as I journey through this pilgrim land to reach my eternal home with You. This world is not my natural home. I am only passing through. Remind me my citizenship is in Heaven. In Jesus' name, amen.

Never Empty-Handed

"And I will give this people favor in the sight of the Egyptians; and it shall be, when you go, that you shall not go empty-handed" (Exod. 3:21).

READ: EXODUS 3:21-22

The happy children ran along the blue shores of the ocean, searching for seashells in the early morning hours. The white-crested waves had washed up a fabulous treasure from the previous night. The children were the first to plunder the sandy shores and claim the abundance of the sea. They gleefully gathered the loot of precious gems. Then, filling their hands with bounty more precious to them than gold, they laughed with delight.

The children of Israel found favor with the Egyptians when Moses led the Israelites out of slavery. The Promised Land offered the hope of freedom from slavery and affliction. But more importantly, the Israelites would be free to worship God in this new land.

The journey to the Promised Land required resources, but the people would not go empty-handed on the journey. So, God told Moses in Exodus 3:22, "But every woman shall ask of her neighbor, namely, of her who dwells near her house, articles of silver, articles of gold, and clothing; and you shall put *them* on your sons and on your daughters. So you shall plunder the Egyptians."

God provided for His people. He does the same for us today. We will never go empty-handed when we place our life in His hands. He supplies all the needs of those who rely on Him as their Source.

THOUGHT FOR THE DAY
Lord, like the children of Israel, make me a vessel to receive Your abundant blessings.

PRAYER
Lord, let me constantly be reminded that You will never fail me, that You are always there for me, and that You will provide for my needs—spiritual and physical—when I place my trust in You. In Jesus' name, amen.

Get Ready for Your Miracle

"God also bearing witness both with signs and wonders, with various miracles, and gifts of the Holy Spirit, according to His own will" (Heb. 2:4).

READ: HEBREWS 2:4-18

The car careened through the curve and hit a fence when the driver dodged an oncoming speeding vehicle. Although no one was hurt, an unborn baby entered this world prematurely. After the little girl's birth, the doctor commented on how black and blue the baby was. It was a miracle the baby had survived with no permanent damage.

Have you experienced a miracle, or are you still awaiting your miracle? God is not short on miracles. He is ever ready to meet you at your greatest need. God has abundant signs, wonders, and miracles beyond the human imagination. People and circumstances prove God is willing and able to bring to fruition wonders and miracles of which we can only dream. Science may fail us, but God never will. We only need to believe and wait in anticipation for God to work on our behalf. He is eager to provide.

THOUGHT FOR THE DAY

Don't limit God with your expectations. Instead, allow Him to perform His miracles, healings, and wonders through His limitless and loving provision.

PRAYER

Heavenly Father, thank You for all the times You were there for me—healing me and miraculously providing for me when, at times, I was not even aware. In Jesus' name, amen.

Envy or Admiration

"For where envy and self-seeking exist, confusion and every evil thing *are there"* (James 3:16).

READ: JAMES 3:14-16

Obsessed by what others have, a little pony found itself filled with envy. Tony the Pony came out of the gate, wishing he was the fastest horse in the race. He envied the horses that ran faster than he. Tony thought his long mane slowed him down. He wanted a short mane like the other horses. So, Tony persuaded his trainer, Mickey, to cut his beautiful, long mane, hoping he would win the Steeplechase Race. But Tony was still slow.

One day, a wealthy man came to the stalls where all the horses were kept, wanting a horse with a long mane. But because Tony now had a short mane, the man didn't choose him, and Tony was sad. If only he had his long, beautiful mane back.

Tony the Pony envied every other horse that had something he didn't. He couldn't be happy with just being himself. His was a sad life, filled with jealousy, envy, and emptiness.

Genesis 37 tells us that Joseph was his father's favorite son. To show his pleasure, Jacob made Joseph a coat of many colors. This obvious display of favoritism caused his other sons to envy Joseph. Joseph salted their wound by sharing dreams of his superiority over his brothers and family. As a result, Joseph's brothers sold him into slavery. Although the account ends with Israel's salvation, suffering and shame fill the account because of envy.

Paul says, "Love suffers long *and* is kind; love does not envy; love does not parade itself, is not puffed up" (1 Cor. 13:4). Love gives instead of takes. Love gives praise and support but doesn't envy or stir up jealousy over what others have.

THOUGHT FOR THE DAY
Envy is a killer. It destroys the ones who strive to outdo others.

PRAYER
Lord, help me be satisfied with who I am, what I have, and what I do. Help me to value others as I exalt them above myself. In Jesus' name, amen.

A Shortcut to Patience

"Therefore we also, since we are surrounded by so great a cloud of witnesses, let us lay aside every weight, and the sin which so easily ensnares us, and let us run with endurance the race that is set before us, looking unto Jesus, the author and finisher of our faith; who for the joy that was set before Him endured the cross, despising the shame, and has sat down at the right hand of the throne of God" (Heb. 12:1-2).

READ: HEBREWS 12:1-3

A little boy had to climb a steep hill to get to his home in the country, so he cut a path through a cemetery to avoid the rough incline. The shortcut made his walk home quicker and more pleasant. This shortcut gave him more time to enjoy the football game with his friends after school. The mountain didn't get the best of him because he outfoxed the problem by "cheating" his way to a better solution.

James, the half-brother of Jesus, says, "Knowing that the testing of your faith produces patience. But let patience have *its* perfect work, that you may be perfect and complete, lacking nothing" (James 1:3-4). That's good advice. When things try our faith, patience becomes necessary. Some never ask God for patience because they know trials will come to put their tolerance to the test. Waiting for the problems to pass requires patience for our faith to grow. One way to wade through those trials is to thank our way through them. Thanking God distracts us from the trials and brings us closer to peace. Reminding ourselves of all the blessings surrounding us also takes our minds off the trials. Refuse to murmur and complain, and instead, turn your thoughts to something for which to be thankful. A glimmer of hope always exists, for which we can be grateful.

THOUGHT FOR THE DAY
Distracting ourselves from our trials and tribulations through thanking God comforts us so that God can bless us despite those trials.

PRAYER
Thank You, Lord, for giving me blessings I don't deserve, even during trials I don't understand. Help me be thankful as I pass through the fiery trials to the other side, where my hope rests in You. In Jesus' name, amen.

Diving Headfirst to the Cross

"For the message of the cross is foolishness to those who are perishing, but to us who are being saved it is the power of God" (1 Cor. 1:18).

READ: 1 CORINTHIANS 1:17-19

A quip on a t-shirt cleverly stated, "I'm left-handed. What is your superpower?" Some nations declare themselves to be a super-power among all countries. Some bodybuilders proclaim themselves a superpower among athletes. Many attempt to achieve superpower status in their field. How do we gain that recognition? And should we even attempt it?

God is where all power begins, belongs, and continues. Ephesians 1:15-23 enumerates God's great power toward us by explaining that God has given believers exceeding power because Christ was raised from the dead and seated at the Father's right hand in heavenly places. This power is "far above all principality and power and might and dominion, and every name that is named, not only in this age but also in that which is to come" (Eph. 1:21). We are merely a conduit through which Christ works. We are the church—the believers in Christ. We are only the branches. Ephesians 1:22-23 describes the power of the Godhead: "And He put all *things* under His feet, and gave Him *to be* head over all *things to the church, which is His body, the fullness of Him who fills all in all." Christ is "the Alpha and the Omega, the* Beginning and *the* End" (Rev. 22:13).

We lay claim to Christ's power and experience salvation by plunging head-first into God's mercy, which He demonstrated through the death of His Son on the cross. Galatians 6:14 says, "But God forbid that I should boast except in the cross of our Lord Jesus Christ, by whom the world has been crucified to me, and I to the world." Humility comes from realizing Christ is our Strength. It is not of our own making. Paul writes, "And He said to me, 'My grace is sufficient for you, for My strength is made perfect in weakness.' Therefore most gladly I will rather boast in my infirmities, that the power of Christ may rest upon me" (2 Cor. 12:9).

THOUGHT FOR THE DAY

Let us humble ourselves before God and believe His power is ours because He provides for us when we trust in Christ, and that alone.

PRAYER

Lord, I believe You are the One to Whom all power belongs. In Jesus' name, amen.

A Sweet Fragrance

"For we are to God the fragrance of Christ among those who are being saved and among those who are perishing" (2 Cor. 2:15).

READ: 2 CORINTHIANS 2:14-17

The perfume scent permeated the air as my niece and I filled the ornate bottles with fragrances. Then, sitting on the front porch steps, we combined various fragrances from the craft kit to make a perfume each of us identified as our own. My young niece proudly declared, "This is the best smelling perfume I've ever had!" The perfume was her signature scent.

God says our prayers are an aroma to Him—our signature scent offered to the Lord. The golden vials full of odors described in Revelation 5:8 are the prayers of the saints. Our heartfelt prayers offered over our lifetime are a gift of praise and thanksgiving to God, just like a fragrant perfume.

Lift your heart and voice to the Lord in prayer. As you do, you create a sweet perfume that has your signature.

THOUGHT FOR THE DAY
Prayers are a sweet-smelling odor to the Lord.

PRAYER
Thank You, Lord, for hearing and answering our prayers when we offer them to You.
In Jesus' name, amen.

Giving Up Your Gods

"Whose end is destruction, whose god is their belly, and whose glory is in their shame—who set their mind on earthly things" (Phil. 3:19).

READ: PHILIPPIANS 3:17-21

The feast was fit for a king—wild duck, champagne, lobster, steak, and desserts. You would think Marie Antoinette was making the toast. Any host would be proud.

I recall the story of a young college girl whose friend offered her a chocolate treat after every meal. At first, the girl declined, but eventually, she succumbed to the chocolate temptations until it became a habit. Over the years, her waist grew along with her appetite as chocolate treats became an addiction. She yearned for the days before the chocolate had become her god.

Maybe food isn't your weakness. Some say, "I eat to live," while others admit, "I live to eat!" Food can become a god we turn to when life throws us a curve, when we're bored, or when it tastes good. Many make sports their god. They never miss a football or basketball game—even when it means missing worship at church. We can even place other pleasure activities first at our altars. Education and careers can also become gods, as can clothes and jewelry. And of course, the good, old money trap is an idol for many. Just can't get enough of a good thing.

Although none of the above is wrong, they become idols when they take God's place. These little gods never satisfy. Exodus 20:3-5 says:

> You shall have no other gods before Me. You shall not make for yourself a carved image—any likeness of *anything* that *is* in heaven above, or that *is* in the earth beneath, or that is in the water under the earth; you shall not bow down to them nor serve them. For I, the LORD your God, *am* a jealous God, visiting the iniquity of the fathers upon the children to the third and fourth *generations* of those who hate Me, but showing mercy to thousands, to those who love Me and keep My commandments.

THOUGHT FOR THE DAY
Little gods slip into our lives stealthily, taking the shape of unknown idols.

PRAYER
Lord, make me aware of temptations that can become bigger than life. Help me resist any that might become an idol in my life. If I fail, restore me as I honor and serve You, the one true God. In Jesus' name, amen.

Are You Meek?

"Blessed are the meek, For they shall inherit the earth" (Matt. 5:5).

READ: MATTHEW 5:2–5

My son proposed on bended knee in a beautiful flower garden to the girl of his dreams. Butterflies gracefully floated by as he did. He waited patiently for her answer, ultimately winning her hand in marriage.

A meek spirit often wins the day. Meek should not be confused with weak. A tranquil and even-tempered disposition best describes the meek person. Patience and a gentle, composed spirit mark them. They are not haughty or arrogant but modest and checked with restraint. A meek person controls their emotions and actions, displaying cool and calm behavior.

Jesus said, "The meek . . . shall inherit the earth" (Matt. 5:5). Being meek doesn't mean we can't shout at a sporting event or applaud victoriously at a graduation ceremony. Nor does meek mean we are a doormat. Those who are weak in their faith would not inherit the earth. The meek are strong, and the strong in faith will receive God's promises. Psalm 37:11 says, "But the meek shall inherit the earth, And shall delight themselves in the abundance of peace."

THOUGHT FOR THE DAY
Let us not confuse the strength of the meek with the lack of the weak.

PRAYER
Lord, let me delve deeper into the meek spirit You exemplified while on earth. In Jesus' name, amen.

The Power of Ordinary People

"Which is manifest evidence of the righteous judgment of God, that you may be counted worthy of the kingdom of God, for which you also suffer" (2 Thess. 1:5).

READ: 2 THESSALONIANS 1:3-7

A Guinness World Record set for the longest day trapped in an elevator—six days—is out of the ordinary. The largest jewelry heist in history—136 million—is also counted among the extraordinary. So are the astounding 133 push-ups in a minute. And the longest-reigning queen is Queen Elizabeth II—over sixty-eight years as of this writing.

Although few ordinary people will ever attain—or desire—these extravagant deeds, God offers us all the opportunity to be extraordinary in the spiritual arena. He requires that we place our lives into His sovereign hands. Ecclesiastes 9:11 says, "I returned and saw under the sun that—The race *is* not to the swift, Nor the battle to the strong, Nor bread to the wise, Nor riches to men of understanding, Nor favor to men of skill; But time and chance happen to them all."

Setting unbelievable records for speed, strength, riches, or skill is not worthy of eternal rewards. What, then, is a worthy endeavor? Paul says, "Therefore if anyone cleanses himself from the latter, he will be a vessel for honor, sanctified and useful for the Master, prepared for every good work" (2 Tim. 2:21). We realize the power of an ordinary person when we put our faith on the line for the One Who died for us, Jesus Christ.

THOUGHT FOR THE DAY
What I desire to achieve is not fame or fortune in this life but the approval of God throughout eternity.

PRAYER
Lord, make me a vessel willing to do Your will. You are Sovereign. My choices reflect where I put my trust. Help me always be submissive to You. Change me from ordinary to extraordinary by placing You foremost in my thoughts, decisions, and actions. In Jesus' name, amen.

Food for Thought

"For 'whoever calls on the name of the Lord shall be saved'" (Rom. 10:13).

READ: ROMANS 10:11-14

I once observed a young toddler sitting with her mother, father, and baby brother at a fast-food restaurant. The family bowed their heads, instructing the little girl to say the blessing over the food. She prayed loudly, "Food! Amen!" The family waited in vain for more. She had made her plea to God and was ready to eat. Even though her prayer was short and sweet, it spoke volumes to the One Who hears the simplest of prayers.

God hears all prayers. Just plain, simple language gets His attention. We are not required to embellish our words, exhibit a good command of our language, speak with flashy words, use an impressive voice, or display strong body language.

Offering a simple prayer also applies when someone approaches God's throne, seeking His forgiveness and approval. Unfortunately, we often complicate salvation with formulas and methods that we believe make it more legitimate. We want people to jump through the hoops of our standards, not God's.

A repentant heart and sincere desire to please the Lord should motivate us to seek His forgiveness. Acts 2:21 states, "And it shall come to pass, *That* whoever calls on the name of the LORD Shall be saved." No one-two-three, a-b-c formula. All that is required is calling, and whoever does will be saved. I can't imagine anything more rewarding.

THOUGHT FOR THE DAY
When devoid of what to pray, a heartfelt plea to the Lord signals our earnestness to seek and please Him. God will save those who call on His name.

PRAYER
Thank You, Lord, for hearing me even when I flounder with words. May I be authentic and straightforward when I approach You—never attempting to impress but seeking to serve and worship You in everything I say and do. In Jesus' name, amen.

Clothed in Christ's Righteousness

"I will greatly rejoice in the Lord, My soul shall be joyful in my God; For He has clothed me with the garments of salvation, He has covered me with the robe of righteousness, As a bridegroom decks himself with ornaments, And as a bride adorns herself with her jewels" (Isa. 61:10).

READ: ISAIAH 61:10-11

White, wispy, flowing chiffon floated around the maiden's ankles as she gathered fragrant-scented lilies from a field where they gently bent their heads in the cool breeze. The young lady dressed in garments that matched the beauty of the flowers she cut. A lovely garland of flowers encircled her long strand of soft, golden curls. Does this sound like a description of a character from a romance novel? To complete the scene, a tall, dark, and handsome young man rode up on a white horse.

As believers, we are the lady described as a bride adorned with her jewels, clothed in garments of salvation, and covered with Christ's robe of righteousness. The tall, dark, handsome hero in the story is like the bridegroom who decks himself with ornaments in the account described in Isaiah 61. Both await a marriage to the King of kings and Lord of lords, Jesus Christ.

Revelation 19:7-9 says:

Let us be glad and rejoice and give Him glory, for the marriage of the Lamb has come, and His wife has made herself ready. And to her it was granted to be arrayed in fine linen, clean and bright, for the fine linen is the righteous acts of the saints. Then he said to me, "Write: Blessed *are* those who are called to the marriage supper of the Lamb!" And he said to me, "These are the true sayings of God."

The clean and bright linen equates to the righteous acts of the saints. Believers are wrapped in the robes of righteousness through the redeeming grace of God through Jesus Christ. Furthermore, Ephesians 6:14 prompts us to "stand therefore, having girded your waist with truth, having put on the breastplate of righteousness." This breastplate covers our hearts. Let the righteousness of God protect your heart.

THOUGHT FOR THE DAY
The righteousness of God comes from believing, knowing, and living a life in Christ.

PRAYER
Lord, surround and infuse me with Your righteousness. I pray for You to clothe me in the righteousness of Christ. In Jesus' name, amen.

Brute Force

"And from the days of John the Baptist until now the kingdom of heaven suffers violence, and the violent take it by force" (Matt. 11:12).

READ: MATTHEW 11:7-15

My nephew experienced culture shock when he journeyed to Kenya on a mission trip. In our country, he traveled on expansive infrastructures of highways, but there, he traveled to villages over brushy, rutted pig trails. The loudest voice—or sheer brute force—determined the outcome of a traffic accident. Fighting might even break out. Often, if a foreigner was involved in an accident, the judgment favored the hometown boy.

My nephew remembers walking with the local pastor in the city when a muscular native, a giant of a man, approached them, holding a heavy chain. At the end of the chain was a laughing hyena. The pastor explained that this was the town's "hit" man and the hyena his weapon of choice—the primitive weapon of a bounty hunter. He would unleash the savage animal on his victim. There was no justice system.

The Kingdom of Heaven was met with brute force when an unruly mob forced Jesus into judgment. Innocent and sinless, He challenged darkness and won. We are promised eternal life by believing in Him and His substitutionary death. "We are more than conquerors through [Christ]" (Rom. 8:37).

THOUGHT FOR THE DAY
Let us be bold and brave in our journey through life.

PRAYER
Lord, in my daily walk with You, remind me You are on my side. Knowing this, I am equipped for whatever circumstances I encounter. In Jesus' name, amen.

Desperate for God

"Do you not know that you are the temple of God and that the Spirit of God dwells in you" (1 Cor. 3:16)?

READ: 1 CORINTHIANS 3:7-17

Considering an investment? What would it be? Real estate, the stock market, gold, bitcoin, or the latest monetary exchange? Perhaps you would invest in a college education, a fancy house, an exotic vacation, or a red sports car. The possibilities are limitless. But if we wish to make a wise investment, we will invest all we have in a relationship with God.

Our Creator God invested Himself in us. When Jesus went to the cross, suffered, died a cruel death, and rose from the dead, He invested totally in us. He left the perfect realm of Heaven so that the imperfect human race could receive the most significant investment of all time: salvation. Salvation equips us to spend eternity with a loving God and His only begotten Son, Jesus Christ. In Revelation 21:2-4, John describes eternal salvation best:

> Then I, John, saw the holy city, New Jerusalem, coming down out of heaven from God, prepared as a bride adorned for her husband. And I heard a loud voice from heaven saying, "Behold, the tabernacle of God *is* with men, and He will dwell with them, and they shall be His people. God Himself will be with them *and be* their God. And God will wipe away every tear from their eyes; there shall be no more death, nor sorrow, nor crying. There shall be no more pain, for the former things have passed away."

When we become desperate enough to immerse ourselves thoroughly into the will and ways of God, we make the ultimate investment. When we give our all to our Creator, He never disappoints.

THOUGHT FOR THE DAY
God supplied everything we could ever need when He sent Jesus to die for our sins. The Holy Spirit now indwells us. We will lack nothing when we invest our lives in God's will.

PRAYER
Lord, make me desperate for You. I don't want to be content with the status quo. Shake me up spiritually so that I am ignited for You. In Jesus' name, amen.

Will God Wait?

"Therefore, the Lord will wait, that He may be gracious to you; And therefore, He will be exalted, that He may have mercy on you. For the Lord is a God of justice; Blessed are all those who wait for Him" (Isa. 30:18).

READ: ISAIAH 30:18-19

I have learned God is not in a hurry. He measures time with a different device than we do, viewing our twenty-four-hour cycle differently. Peter writes, "But, beloved, do not forget this one thing, that with the Lord one day *is* as a thousand years, and a thousand years as one day" (2 Peter 3:8).

Can our calendar be marked with pauses as God waits for our benefit? Yes, God waits in the thrones of Heaven to mark the salvation of souls. Isaiah assures us God waits. He waits for us so that He might be merciful to us. God is a just God. He doesn't judge without first allowing time for people to accept Him.

We, too, must be patient with our loved ones as God draws them to Him. Never in a hurry to judge the unrighteous, God patiently waits for people to accept His Son, Jesus Christ. But God will not wait forever. Eventually, we must decide whether to accept Christ or not. Patience in waiting for the salvation of loved ones is a godly trait we should adopt. While we wait for them to decide, we can pray for them.

THOUGHT FOR THE DAY
The Lord waits for those to seek and accept Him.

PRAYER
As I wait, remind me that You, too, Lord, are patiently waiting with an everlasting love.
In Jesus' name, amen.

Bind Doubt and Unbelief

"Immediately the father of the child cried out and said with tears, 'Lord, I believe; help my unbelief'" (Mark 9:24).

READ: MARK 9:16-27

Have you ever been in tears? The father in this account was. A mute spirit plagued his son, causing him to convulse uncontrollably. Sometimes, the convulsions almost killed the boy. The father was desperate for the Lord's touch. He took his deep anguish and need for a miracle to Jesus. I imagine he choked on his words when he told Jesus about his son's illness. Finally, desperation drove him to confront the issue and seek help from a miracle-working Jesus.

Jesus told this father his son would be made whole if he believed. "Jesus said to him . . . 'All things *are* possible to him who believes'" (Mark 9:23). Not just some things, but all things. The child's father cried through tears, "'Lord, I believe; help my unbelief!'"

We are sometimes like this father—filled with unbelief. When you sense unbelief rearing its ugly head, nip it in the bud. Admit you have unbelief, then defeat it by asking God for help. Only by submission to Him can you believe and receive.

THOUGHT FOR THE DAY
Doubt is common when things seem impossible. When doubt enters, admit you can't believe. Then ask God to help you believe.

PRAYER
Lord, help me admit my failings and to ask You for the ability to believe for my miracle. In Jesus' name, amen.

Fingerprints of God

"For, behold, I create new heavens and a new earth; And the former shall not be remembered, or come into mind" (Isa. 65:17).

READ: ISAIAH 65:17-25

The fingerprints of God express His magnificent creation. God formed all nature simply by speaking it into existence. Evolution did not form it; test tubes did not create it. Almighty God Himself created it.

Revelation 21:1-7 says:

Now I saw a new heaven and a new earth, for the first heaven and the first earth had passed away. Also there was no more sea. Then I, John, saw the holy city, New Jerusalem, coming down out of heaven from God, prepared as a bride adorned for her husband. And I heard a loud voice from heaven saying, "Behold, the tabernacle of God *is* with men, and He will dwell with them, and they shall be His people. God Himself will be with them *and be* their God. And God will wipe away every tear from their eyes; there shall be no more death, nor sorrow, nor crying. There shall be no more pain, for the former things have passed away." Then He who sat on the throne said, "Behold, I make all things new." And He said to me, "Write, for these words are true and faithful." And He said to me, "It is done! I am the Alpha and the Omega, the Beginning and the End. I will give of the fountain of the water of life freely to him who thirsts. He who overcomes shall inherit all things, and I will be his God and he shall be My son."

We can only imagine God's majesty.

THOUGHT FOR THE DAY
I stand amazed at God's creation.

PRAYER
*Lord, I long for that city where You reign as King of kings and Lord of lords.
In Jesus' name, amen.*

A Wow Moment

"But as it is written, Eye has not seen, nor ear heard, Nor have entered into the heart of man, The things which God has prepared for those who love Him" (1 Cor. 2:9).

READ: 1 CORINTHIANS 2:9-12

A spectacular display of fireworks bursting across the night sky, a group of dolphins streaming through the blue ocean, a waterfall splashing from great heights to the rocky crags below, the sweet taste of honey passing our lips, the joy brought by a huge stash of money. These all stroke our senses and lift our spirits. Moments in our life that bring joy and satisfaction stand out.

But the perfect "wow" moment is when we receive our great reward: our eternal home we will share with God—the moment when we leave our troubles here below and step into our heavenly home where we will dwell forever with the King of glory and experience joy, love, and peace. Abundance and plenty will fill our hearts as we consider His goodness, mercy, and love. His presence will continually indwell us with forgiveness, mercy, peace, love, and joy. And that is only the beginning. The lovingkindness of God stretches our imagination and knows no bounds.

THOUGHT FOR THE DAY
Precious are the treasures that await the believer in our heavenly home.

PRAYER
Heavenly Father, I delight in the hope of Heaven and an eternity spent with You. Your promises to those who believe in You are immeasurable. Waves of joy fill my soul. Be magnified. In Jesus' name, amen.

His Overwhelming Glory

"The heavens declare the glory of God; And the firmament shows His handiwork" (Psalm 19:1).

READ: PSALM 19:1-4

Peeking from the early morning light, the beautiful blue flowers known as morning glories lived up to their name. They created a glorious sight as hundreds of them cascaded over the fence surrounding the little country cottage.

Many of the psalms pronounce the glory of God displayed throughout the heavens. The heavens show His handiwork as a gifted artist would display his talent with canvas and paint. We only need to look around to see the beautiful creation made by our marvelous Creator. God's creation has a spectacular display of nature that awes and inspires. Peace comes from seeing a beautiful sunset and the good sense of knowing Whom to thank. Our Heavenly Father designed a complex but orchestrated universe that goes beyond mere chance.

Some have compared the Divine design of the universe to a finely crafted watch. To assume we could toss intricate parts into the air and see them come together to form a working thing capable of accurately keeping time is absurd. So, too, with the universe. The order and structure reflect a well-thought-out plan. To assume something other than a Divine Creator produced it is blind reasoning and causes us to put our faith in random odds. Our surroundings testify to the grand and powerful designs of God. His overwhelming glory speaks volumes to our minute human nature.

THOUGHT FOR THE DAY

God is in the details. He moves and surrounds us totally with His awe-inspiring creation.

PRAYER

Lord, thank You for Your gift to me. Throughout the universe, I see Your grand display of creation. In Jesus' name, amen.

God's Compliment

"And when He had removed him, He raised up for them David as king, to whom also He gave testimony and said, 'I have found David the son of Jesse, a man after My own heart, who will do all My will'" (Acts 13:22).

READ: ACTS 13:18-22

Some have a real knack for complimenting others. They pass on cheer and joy like breath mints at a dentists' convention for everything from purple hairstyles to smothered liver. They just have a way of making others feel good with their words.

Compliments lift the spirit of the recipient. A compliment must resound with sincerity to be an honest gift of the heart. Recognizing one's outstanding performance or excellent behavior uplifts and reinforces them. Compliments promote the prosperity of the soul and fuel a positive self-image by encouraging us, motivating better behavior, and stirring us onward. A genuine compliment for a job well done galvanizes and stimulates us to greater action.

God complimented David, king of Israel. Although David made many blunders, failed in moral living, and sinned grossly, the Lord identified him as a man after God's heart. The Lord looked past David's failures. God saw David's imperfections, but He also saw a repentant heart that longed for forgiveness and restitution from a holy God. David's adultery and subsequent murder of the man whom he had defied in his immoral actions laid heavily upon David's mind. He chose to forsake his past and live a life that pleased God.

God honored David's repentance and viewed him from a unique perspective—not judging his past but honoring the person David became, a man determined to please the Lord. As a result, David finished strong by living his remaining days by pleasing the Lord, which led to him receiving a phenomenal compliment from God.

THOUGHT FOR THE DAY
Although I am sure to fail at times, I desire to please God and do His will in all I attempt.

PRAYER
Lord, help me keep my failures to a minimum, repent when needed, and strive to live a life pleasing to You in everything I do. In Jesus' name, amen.

Be Significant

"But you shall receive power when the Holy Spirit has come upon you; and you shall be witnesses to Me in Jerusalem, and in all Judea and Samaria, and to the end of the earth" (Acts 1:8).

READ: ACTS 1:7-8

Feeling worthless? Such was the attitude of a young boy after his parents had continuously told him he wouldn't amount to anything. Sure enough, when he reached adulthood, he did poorly. Success for him entailed being a failure as he lived up to his parents' expectations. His parents had tagged him with a label that formed his misdirected behavior throughout life. But God saw his value. Although deemed worthless by others, God valued him. He was loved and treasured by the Creator of the universe. God's love is so complete that even though we are sinners, God sent His Son to die for us.

Regardless of our station in life, God values us. Our Creator extends His love to each person and has a vested interest in every person's life. He cares and is ready to receive those considered "worthless" by the world.

Every person is unique. We each have something to offer that no other person has. We have a smile, a compliment, and a talent that is ours alone. God wants us to use our special uniqueness for Him . . . to be significant. We can give from our hearts and bless others in ways only we can. We are rich in our own traits, unlike anyone else, and we should use those traits to edify Christ. God wants us to put forth our best effort and conduct ourselves, so we magnify His love to those we meet.

In Acts 5:14-15, we read, "Believers were increasingly added to the Lord, multitudes of both men and women, so that they brought the sick out into the streets and laid *them* on beds and couches, that at least the shadow of Peter passing by might fall on some of them."

We can serve as a conduit for the outflow of Spirit-empowered love and forgiveness by displaying God's love in tangible ways. Start with faith, then pray and let God lead. Next, share the Good News of God's love and forgiveness.

THOUGHT FOR THE DAY

Our footprint on this planet impacts others when we act in God's love, mercy, and forgiveness.

PRAYER

Thank You, God, that Your Son embraced the lowest, the least, and the lost with overwhelming love and acceptance. Help me make an impact on those who are suffering. Help me become love in action.
In Jesus' name, amen.

The Elect Lady

"The Elder, to the elect lady and her children, whom I love in the truth, and not only I, but also all those who have known the truth" (2 John 1:1).

READ: 2 JOHN 1:1-5, 13

This Scripture has always baffled me. I've often wondered who the elect lady was. She seems to be a mother because John acknowledges she has children. In verse thirteen, John mentions, "The children of your elect sister greet you, Amen." Is she an aunt? The Bible addresses many women by name, but for some reason, John avoids identifying her. From his description, we also know she espouses the truth, which is her identifying trait. An entire book of the New Testament is addressed to this elect lady.

I have also questioned what made her elect, so I consulted the word's original meaning as used in the Bible. The word in Greek means "favorite or chosen." The definition does not mean she was necessarily elected to a public office. Nor does it suggest she possessed any talent such as singing, acting, or drawing. She is not even paid homage for loyalty—as was Ruth in the Old Testament—nor for her bravery—such as Queen Esther, who saved the Jews from destruction.

The trait of truth she possessed can be developed and maintained in all of us. First, we must strongly desire God's truth and lean on the Holy Spirit to show us that truth. Then, we must commit all we have to know and live out that truth in all sincerity as God expresses it in Scripture.

When we apply the Word, the truth of God, we resemble the elect lady. We are specially marked when we immerse ourselves in the truth, just as the elect lady was.

THOUGHT FOR THE DAY
God chooses the elect person to live out the truth in all their ways.

PRAYER
"Lord, make me an elect and chosen vessel, living for You and proclaiming Your truth so that I might glorify You. In Jesus' name, amen.

Is It Everything or Just Adequate?

"So then, because you are lukewarm, and neither cold nor hot, I will vomit you out of My mouth" (Rev. 3:16).

READ: REVELATION 3:15-16

Hot tea, anyone? Or perhaps, you prefer a tall glass of Southern sweet tea filled to the brim with crushed ice. Either way suits your fancy for whatever your preferences might be at the time. But we object to anything lukewarm. Temperature matters. Our taste pallet responds favorably to the two extremes, but never to lukewarm. We are not prepared to accept average temperatures.

The Laodiceans, however, were a group of people Christ described as tepid, objectionable, lukewarm, and undesirable. The overall image is a group of lackadaisical people. They were not sold out to the highest degree. Jesus compared them to a glass of liquid made undesirable by its temperature. Because they are lukewarm, Christ would spew them out of His mouth. The Laodiceans did not treat Jesus as an honored guest or worthy of their effort.

To avoid being like the Laodiceans, we should follow the example of what we hear in Revelation 5:12-13:

> Worthy is the Lamb who was slain To receive power and riches and wisdom, And strength and honor and glory and blessing. And every creature which is in heaven and on the earth and under the earth and such as are in the sea, and all that are in them, I heard saying: "Blessing and honor and glory and power *Be* to Him who sits on the throne, And to the Lamb, forever and ever!"

Our entire being should lean toward the Savior who redeemed us through His shed blood on Calvary, desiring to immerse our lives in Him.

THOUGHT FOR THE DAY
Our natural bent is sometimes to our self-interest. Let us make God our all-in-all and treat Him as our most honored Savior and Lord. Let us make Jesus our everything.

PRAYER
Never let me be delayed or destroyed by distractions but always on fire for You, Lord. Help me make You my everything—more than simply enough, more than merely adequate, my everything. In Jesus' name, amen.

Those Who Wait on the Lord

"And while he was still talking with them, there was the messenger, coming down to him; and then the king said, 'Surely this calamity is from the Lord; why should I wait for the Lord any longer'" (2 Kings 6:33).

READ: 2 KINGS 6:30-33

We all waste time—the one commodity of which we are allotted only so much. Often, we don't willingly waste it, but circumstances, such as waiting in lines at the grocery store, lounging in a doctor's office waiting room, waiting for an elevator, or waiting for downloads on a computer for us to lose that time. Estimates say we spend an average of nine to fifteen minutes waiting at stop lights and traffic signs. Waiting in traffic jams for hours on the freeways is common for those living in large cities. The average seventy-year-old person has wasted approximately three years waiting.

We may also grow impatient waiting for Jesus to return. Feeling cheated of an immediate victory, we may drop our faith walk and become discouraged. Once close to God, we may gravitate toward lethargy. We must beware of spiritual despondency by reassessing our spiritual goals and renewing our strength in the Lord.

Waiting on the Lord does not mean we must waste our time until He returns. Isaiah 40:31 says, "But those who wait upon the Lord Shall renew *their* strength; They shall mount up with wings as eagles. They shall run and not be weary; they shall walk and not faint."

THOUGHT FOR THE DAY
As I wait for Jesus' return, I will fill my days with sweet expectancy and godly enthusiasm.

PRAYER
Teach me, Lord, to wait—not waste. In Jesus' name, amen.

To the Core of Our Being

"You shall love the LORD your God with all your heart, with all your soul, and with all your strength" (Deut. 6:5).

READ: DEUTERONOMY 6:5-9

"How do I love thee? Let me count the ways. I love thee to the depth and breadth and height My soul can reach," said Elizabeth Barrett Browning. She declared her love for her husband with the passion of her breath, smiles, tears—her entire being—finally concluding that if God willed it, she would love her husband even better after death.

Moses tells us in Deuteronomy 6 that our love for God must embrace a passion that includes our heart, soul, and strength. We must give our love with everything we've got, nothing short of total devotion and love to our glorious Heavenly Father, Creator of the universe. For the believer who does this, God promises He will "dwell with them, and they shall be His people. God Himself will be with them *and be* their God" (Rev. 21:3). John also writes, "Let us be glad and rejoice and give Him glory, for the marriage of the Lamb has come, and His wife has made herself ready" (Rev. 19:7).

Our enemy, Satan, is vehemently opposed to our spiritual marriage with Christ Jesus. Believers, however, are blessed in holy matrimony with the One Who gives life eternal. And we will love Him even greater on the eternal side, completely comprehending and fully realizing His love for us.

THOUGHT FOR THE DAY
Love beyond degree from God above reached humanity on the cross of Calvary.

PRAYER
Lord, I desire to return the love You have extended to me with a love that goes to the core of my being. I want to love You with all my heart, soul, and strength. In Jesus' name, amen.

God Enables

"Now He who establishes us with you in Christ and has anointed us is God" (2 Cor. 1:21).

READ: 2 CORINTHIANS 1:20-22

When my son attempted to ride his bike without training wheels, my husband held the back of the seat, supporting him as he pedaled. Usually, this entailed riding in large circles on our back driveway. After holding him up for a period, he told our son he would give him a quarter if he tried by himself. His response was, "I don't want your old quarter!" Soon, my husband let him go alone. He rode without assistance and made the large circle. It surprised our son to see he was riding without help. His dad said, "Keep doing what you're doing."

Just as my husband enabled our son to ride a bike by himself, God enables us to live for Him. Paul says in 2 Corinthians 3:5, "Not that we are sufficient of ourselves to think of anything as *being* from ourselves, but our sufficiency *is* from God." God's grace enables us to live self-controlled, upright, and godly lives. He enables us to live a life of integrity, denying worldly lusts and sinful pleasures. We are no longer slaves to sin but are free in Christ.

God's grace also brings us salvation individually when we believe in Christ. We hope for eternal life, which God promised before time began (Titus 1:1-4). Jesus said in John 3:17, "For God did not send his Son into the world to condemn the world, but that the world through Him might be saved."

When we fail with our efforts, we can turn to the God Who provides. The Christian path of obedience is paved with God's provision when we rely on His willingness and ability to direct our steps. He is a great God Who created and keeps the universe. Furthermore, He can sustain us in our daily walk with Him.

THOUGHT FOR THE DAY
God is willing and able to orchestrate the entire universe and demonstrate His power in my finite life when I turn it over to Him.

PRAYER
Lord, direct my steps, lead my path, and guide my ways as I go through life depending upon You. In Jesus' name, amen.

From Information to Action

"But be doers of the word, and not hearers only, deceiving yourselves" (James 1:22).

READ: JAMES 1:22-25

Leveling up. You know the Scripture and love learning more of it, devouring it eagerly. Or perhaps, you rush through your Bible readings rather than meditating on them. For those who want a fuller and deeper understanding of God's will, the Word reveals and enlightens. Getting a grasp of the essence of the Bible in our minds grows our faith. Furthermore, praying the Word of God puts teeth into our Bible study. Praying the Word establishes the truth of God over all situations and circumstances. Doubt is diminished, and understanding comes to light.

But what next? Do we allow the Scripture to lie dormant, or do we apply the Word to our real life? Second Chronicles 6:17 instructs, "And now, O LORD God of Israel, let Your word come true, which You have spoken to Your servant David." David anchors his plea for the faithful, unvarnished Word in his belief in and love for God. David's desire for the truth abounded in his delight in the Word of God. Likewise, our desire to see God's truth manifests itself when we move from information to action on what we know from Scripture.

Jesus taught in Matthew 4:4, "But He answered and said, 'It is written, Man shall not live by bread alone, but by every word that proceeds from the mouth of God.'" *Live* is an action and shows movement and momentum. It is not stagnant. We do not experience life as though it were passing us by on a large movie screen. We truly live for God when we meditate on Scripture, pray the Word of God over people and circumstances, and apply what we've learned.

THOUGHT FOR THE DAY
Where I live in deed and action and what I do with my knowledge of Scripture make a difference when I apply the Word of God.

PRAYER
Lord, help me put into action my belief in You as I know and trust You through Scripture so that I can "be [a doer] of the word and not [a hearer] only" (James 1:22). In Jesus' name, amen.

Failure Is Not Final

"Then Samson called to the Lord, saying, 'O Lord God, remember me, I pray! Strengthen me, I pray, just this once, O God, that I may with one blow take vengeance on the Philistines for my two eyes'" (Judges 16:28).

READ: JUDGES 16:4-30

We cheer heroes such as Superman and Batman, the superheroes of movies and theaters. But perhaps, we, too, long for superpowers to rid the world of crime.

Samson was a biblical hero who saved his people. His father, Manoah, prayed to the Lord, asking for guidance to teach him and his wife what to do for their coming baby. "Manoah said, 'Now let Your words come *to pass*! What will be the boy's rule of life and his work?' So, the Angel of the LORD said to Manoah, 'Of all that I said to the woman let her be careful'" (Judges 13:12-13). The angel instructed that no razor should come upon Samson's head, for the child would be a Nazarite to God from the womb and begin to deliver Israel.

Although Samson was blessed and aided Israel, he later fell into temptation and failed God when he told Delilah where his strength lay. The Philistines had paid her to discover the secret. They then shaved his head, gouged out his eyes, and imprisoned him.

At one time a strong and able leader, Samson became a failure but not for long. As the hair on his head grew, he regained his strength. God waited in the shadows to restore him. Although he failed, he was not a failure. God embraced him and once more blessed him. As Samson pushed the temple pillars, the upper level and all who were on it fell upon him. He killed more of Israel's enemies in his death than he did during his life. He was once again victorious.

THOUGHT FOR THE DAY
God is waiting for me—loving me unconditionally—even when I fail Him.

PRAYER
Heavenly Father, forgive me when I fail You. Restore and redeem me as You help me move past my mistakes. In Jesus' name, amen.

Examine Your Secret Motives

"For God will bring every work into judgment, Including every secret thing, Whether good or evil" (Eccl. 12:14).

READ: ECCLESIASTES 12:13-14

The Hollywood star thought her secret would never come to light. She paid a significant sum to buy her daughter's entrance to an Ivy League college. Although the mother didn't know whether her daughter would pass the entrance exam, she ensured her daughter would be accepted. Money paid to get her daughter into the elitist world of education seemed the quickest and easiest guarantee of future success.

Many judge such deceit and power plays. Yet those same ones who judge might themselves fall to such a shameful act if given the opportunity. Money sometimes corrupts even the most unaware when giving in to the temptation benefits those they love. A little help, a little boost, or a little nudge in the right direction through cheating or deceit seems harmless. But honest and godly choices are always the right ones.

THOUGHT FOR THE DAY
Erring on the wrong side through deceit or dishonesty never leaves one with a right relationship with God.

PRAYER
Lord, make me aware of my choices with Your Word so that I might not sin against You. In Jesus' name, amen.

Bucket List

"In all your ways acknowledge Him, And He shall direct your paths" (Prov. 3:6).

READ: PROVERBS 3:5-9

Have you ever thought about what you want to see, do, or purchase before your last breath? Your list might include spending the night in a real castle, walking along the Great Wall of China, visiting an ice castle in Sweden, buying a red Ferrari, or owning a luxurious yacht. Or perhaps, it includes writing a song, attending culinary school, painting a picture, naming a star, or skydiving from an airplane. These exciting adventures may be worth pursuing and bring great pleasure, too.

Yet, the most incredible goal is to live for Christ and point others to Him. By doing this, we express the true spirit of love. To love God and others is the mark of accomplishment. First John 4:16 shows us the most important goal: "And we have known and believed the love that God has for us. God is love, and he who abides in love abides in God, and God in him." John 13:34 teaches us, "A new commandment I give to you, that you love one another; as I have loved you, that you also love one another."

In pursuing our life's dreams, we must remember what defines actual worth. Philippians 3:14 says, "I press toward the goal for the prize of the upward call of God in Christ Jesus." Paul continues, "Our citizenship is in heaven, from which we also eagerly wait for the Savior, the Lord Jesus Christ, who will transform our lowly body that it may be conformed to His glorious body, according to the working by which He is able even to subdue all things to Himself" (Phil. 3:20-21).

THOUGHT FOR THE DAY

While exciting adventures thrill us, true joy comes from loving and serving God and sharing this love with others.

PRAYER

I agree with Paul in Philippians 4:11: "Not that I speak in regard to need, for I have learned in whatever state I am, to be content." Lord, may I satisfy myself in loving You and loving others. In Jesus' name, amen.

"O Lord, I pray, please let Your ear be attentive to the prayer of Your servant, and to the prayer of Your servants who desire to fear Your name; and let Your servant prosper this day, I pray, and grant him mercy in the sight of this man. For I was the king's cupbearer" (Neh. 1:11).

READ: NEHEMIAH 1:10-11

Many of us have observed the blind tests on television commercials where random people drink sodas to determine the best-tasting drinks in a competition between major brands. However, in ancient days, the king's cupbearer tasted a king's drink to ensure it was not poisonous. If the cupbearer died, he had saved the king.

Similarly, Jesus Christ was our taste-tester, the One Who saves us from eternal destruction. He willingly took the cup of sin's poison and drank it in our place. Matthew 26:27-28 says, "Then He took the cup, and gave thanks, and gave it to them, saying, 'Drink from it, all of you. For this is my blood of the new covenant, which is shed for many for the remission of sins.'" Through Jesus' death and resurrection, He delivered us from sin's grip. We are saved from the awful death of sin. Romans 6:22-23 says, "But now having been made free from sin, and having become slaves of God, you have your fruit to holiness, and the end, everlasting life. For the wages of sin *is* death; but the gift of God *is* eternal life in Jesus Christ our Lord." Our faith in the actions of Jesus Christ exempts us from an eternal hell.

THOUGHT FOR THE DAY
The poison of sin was taken to the cross by Jesus Christ. Because of His willing death, believers have eternal life.

PRAYER
Thank You, Lord, for the redemption I receive because of Your death. Remind me that Your blood, which was shed for the remission of sins, is the new covenant that provides eternal life and exceeds my expectations. I am thankful for the bitter cup You drank so I can live and be blessed. Your death upon the cross paves the way of mercy for me. In Jesus' name, amen.

"Nor is there salvation in any other, for there is no other name under heaven given among men by which we must be saved" (Acts 4:12).

READ: ACTS 4:8-12

"Man overboard!" shouts a panicky tourist on an ocean cruise. A crew member quickly throws a flotation device out to sea, hoping to rescue the person. A lifebuoy provides a means of salvation from dangerous waters for one who free-falls into the icy, deep blue. But the lifebuoy must prove itself through various tests before the device makes its way to small and large vessels and swimming pools. Nevertheless, it saves many sinking souls.

In the spiritual arena, Jesus is our Lifebuoy, Who saves us from the icy waters of sin. Nothing can pull us into the depths of death's chilling waters when we cling to Him. Although we may die physically, we have eternal life through Jesus Christ. Jesus says in John 7:38, "He who believes in Me, as the Scripture has said, out of his heart will flow rivers of living water." This living water provides a lifeboat that saves our souls from sin. Romans 6:10 says, "For *the death* that He died, He died to sin once for all; but *the life* that He lives, He lives to God."

Romans 5:20-21 explains our salvation as follows: "Moreover the law entered that the offense might abound. But where sin abounded, grace abounded much more, so that as sin reigned in death, even so grace might reign through righteousness to eternal life through Jesus Christ our Lord." We learned of our sins through the law, but we experience salvation through grace.

THOUGHT FOR THE DAY
No one higher and nothing greater calls us to be saved than that which comes from our Savior, Jesus Christ.

PRAYER
Lord, make me aware of Your love and power to save. Your grace is greater than my sin. Although all have sinned, Your grace surpasses the worst sins ever imagined. Thank You for Your supreme sacrifice on the cross to save us. In Jesus' name, amen.

Rent to Own

"Then He got into one of the boats, which was Simon's, and asked him to put out a little from the land. And He sat down and taught the multitudes from the boat" (Luke 5:3).

READ: LUKE 5:1-10

One can rent to own any number of things by paying monthly payments. Doing this is a modern-day phenomenon that makes it possible to own small and large items, such as sofas and large-screen televisions.

Simon Peter leased his boat to Jesus, Who used it as a platform from which to teach people gathered along the shore. Peter's gift of temporary ownership provided a means of communication. Christ spoke to people who needed hope and reconciliation with the Creator God. Jesus taught the people in a common arena—where they gathered to work, fish, eat, and meet their daily needs. Fishermen washed their nets beside the Lake of Gennesaret after fishing all night. There they heard a message of hope.

Jesus spoke a language the people understood. He met them in the most ordinary way. Simon was generous with his boat. He didn't thrust the anchor deeply into the ground and refuse to offer his beloved boat for the Master's use. Peter helped proclaim God's Word to a group of needy people like us who need a personal Savior. The Word reached across the waters and met the people on their level. Jesus offered hope; it was their choice to receive it.

THOUGHT FOR THE DAY

Giving back to God means offering what He first gives to us. Let us be a vessel God can use to establish His kingdom. Let us provide a platform from which Jesus declares His sovereignty.

PRAYER

Lord, everything I have is Yours—my breath, body, brain, belongings, blessings. I give You my all, holding back nothing. Make me realize I don't lose anything by giving it back to You. You are my Source from which I receive and to Whom I give. In Jesus' name, amen.

Not Ashamed

"For I am not ashamed of the gospel of Christ, for it is the power of God to salvation for everyone who believes, for the Jew first and also for the Greek" (Rom. 1:16).

READ: ROMANS 1:16-19

The young man raced through the prayer in muffled breath as he blessed his food at the fancy restaurant. He wanted to thank the Lord for the food He provided, but he didn't want the attention of fellow diners. After all, what would they think? Better to play it safe than be seen as a religious fanatic.

Paul, formerly called Saul, was not shy in speaking up for Christ. He never hesitated to glorify the Lord in public or private. He understood the power of God, which had transformed his life. At one time, he had persecuted Christians, but since his revelation on the road to Damascus, he was a new man. Acts 9:3-4 records, "As he journeyed, he came near Damascus, and suddenly a light shone around him from heaven. Then he fell to the ground and heard a voice saying, 'Saul, Saul, why are you persecuting Me?'" When Paul asked the voice to identify itself, the voice identified itself as the Lord Jesus. Although blinded for three days, Paul received his sight again. Paul believed and never turned back. Paul endured many trials and tribulations, but he proclaimed the saving power of Jesus, and many discovered salvation because of his testimony. He was not ashamed of the Gospel of Christ, for he knew it held power to save.

THOUGHT FOR THE DAY
In the crowd or alone, let me never be ashamed of what Jesus has done for me.

PRAYER
Lord, thank You for Your sacrifice on my behalf. Let me always be grateful and never ashamed. I want to honor You wherever I go. In Jesus' name, amen.

The Envelope, Please

"For all have sinned and fall short of the glory of God" (Rom. 3:23).

READ: ROMANS 3:21-31

Poised with the world watching expectantly, the emcee announced, "The envelope, please." After a long, breathless pause, he proclaimed, "And the winner is . . . " On Judgment Day, we will also wait expectantly for God to call our name. Will you be a winner? Is your name written in the Lamb's Book of Life?

Believing in Jesus and His death and resurrection brings eternal life and gives us hope. Luke 19:10 states, "For the Son of Man has come to seek and to save that which was lost." We must first realize we are lost. Romans 3:23 says, "For all have sinned and fall short of the glory of God." Knowing that we are imperfect helps us realize we need a sinless Savior. When we put our trust in Him, we have eternal life. Although we must die naturally, God promises us life eternal spiritually.

Jesus' substitutionary death makes it possible for us to live eternally. Acts 16:31 says, "So they said, 'Believe on the Lord Jesus Christ, and you will be saved, you and your household.'" Believe so that if God were to say, "The envelope, please," you would be counted among the winners.

THOUGHT FOR THE DAY
It's possible for me to be a winner.

PRAYER
Thank You, Lord, for choosing me. In Jesus' name, amen.

Obeying on Command

"And the LORD commanded us to observe all these statutes, to fear the LORD our God, for our good always, that He might preserve us alive, as it is this day" (Deut. 6:24).

READ: DEUTERONOMY 6:1-25

My niece exclaimed, "Dad took Pearl, our dog, to obedience school, and Dad flunked out! Pearl was able to perform the commands, but Dad wasn't."

Are you willing to obey God and do His commands? Following the Lord offers a promise. When we obey, God promises us long life. Things will go well when we obey God. Showing God respect through obedience ensures we will please Him in whatever we do. Additionally, God will deliver on His promises.

God commands us to love Him with all our heart, soul, and might. Doing so demands total commitment in good and bad times. But how do we love God this way? We determine to submit to His will through thick and thin. We completely surrender to His will and comply with His laws and commandments.

Total commitment secures a relationship that pleases God and is a goal worthy of achieving. The benefits are boundless.

THOUGHT FOR THE DAY
As I bow my will to God's, my life pleases Him and me.

PRAYER
Lord, as I look to You, help me surrender all. In Jesus' name, amen.

The Candy After a Conversation

"Then the multitudes who went before and those who followed cried out, saying: 'Hosanna to the Son of David! Blessed is He who comes in the name of the Lord! Hosanna in the highest'" (Matt. 21:9).

READ: MATTHEW 21:8-9

The telephone conversation ambled on. Little was accomplished. Although much was said, nothing sparked a hearty attitude or a conclusion for either of us—until the last line perked my attention. The lady on the other end of the phone said these little words, "Y'all have a blessed day." Her Southern accent made the words richer—like candy after a ration of sweets.

What a blessing. Just five little words. A conversation wrapped in boredom and steeped with lackluster suddenly became a brilliant jewel. To end a conversation with a blessing is a sweet, generous gesture—a gift that endears the heart. And it was an offer I wanted to accept. This blessing never fails to inspire me and make a difference in my attitude.

Proverbs 31:26 tells us about the power of the tongue: "She opens her mouth with wisdom, And on her tongue is the law of kindness." What blessings we give when we use our tongue to glorify God and show kindness to others.

THOUGHT FOR THE DAY
The power of the tongue can be a great tool to bless.

PRAYER
Lord, help me use words that flow with sincerity and gratitude as I pour out blessings to You and others. In Jesus' name, amen.

Renewing Your Covenant with God

"Likewise He also took the cup after supper, saying, 'This cup is the new covenant in My blood, which is shed for you'" (Luke 22:20).

READ: LUKE 22:13-20

My husband and I have celebrated over forty years of marriage. We have shared many joys as well as sorrows in that time. Our covenant with one another has been tested repeatedly—still, love prevails. Many commemorate milestone anniversaries by renewing their wedding vows. Likewise, we may renew our commitment to Christ to celebrate our spiritual covenant. In response to His faithfulness to us, we may express our love to Him through a new devotion. This covenant represents a bond and refers to the blood covenant that brought our unity. Jesus' death on the cross makes it possible for the Divine Creator to accept us. His blood signifies our redemption. He presented Himself to the Father as a worthy and perfect sacrifice for our sins. God has accomplished His part in the covenant, and once we accept His Son, God's Spirit seals the covenant.

If time has weathered you spiritually, reflect upon God's faithfulness to you. Refresh yourself spiritually. Celebrate the covenant with God with renewed energy and desire.

THOUGHT FOR THE DAY
I am reminded of Jesus' great sacrifice for me upon the cross of Calvary.

PRAYER
Lord, I count my blessings. With renewed devotion, I take my faith to the next level.
In Jesus' name, amen.

The Cliffhanger

"For me to live is Christ, and to die is gain" (Phil. 1:21).

READ: HEBREWS 9:27 AND PHILIPPIANS 1:21

Have you ever watched a television show that ended in a cliffhanger? You worry if the hero will make it. Perhaps you have been in a tight situation and wondered if you would make it. Will your finances be enough to meet your needs? Can you remain married in stressful times? Will science find a cure for your illness?

Although we don't know how much time we have left on earth, we can live with the hope of Heaven. Earth is not the end of our life's story. We must live in light of eternity. Our choices today determine our eternity. While we don't know what the future holds, we do know Who holds the future.

We begin to live when Jesus comes into our life. Our future home in Heaven holds freedom from our current pain, sickness, sorrow, stress, and grief. Revelation 21:4 says, "And God will wipe away every tear from their eyes; there shall be no more death, nor sorrow, nor crying. There shall be no more pain, for the former things have passed away."

THOUGHT FOR THE DAY
Life doesn't end at death but begins with newness in Christ Jesus.

PRAYER
Lord, prepare for me a home in Heaven. In Jesus' name, amen.

It Doesn't Have to Be Easy

"But Jesus looked at them *and said to them, 'With men this is impossible, but with God all things are possible" (Matt. 19:26).*

READ: MATTHEW 19:23–26

My ninety-year-old aunt often said, "It doesn't have to be easy . . . just possible." What a powerful truth. Many have overcome obstacles by applying this thought to their actions. Achieving often takes strength and deliberate determination, but, at times, it requires more than determination—it takes God's help. Everything we do needs God's help. Even the breath we breathe depends on Him.

Hebrews 11:27 recounts Moses' story: "By faith he forsook Egypt, not fearing the wrath of the king: for he endured as seeing Him who is invisible." Moses endured social challenges, physical challenges, and life-threatening challenges from Pharaoh. His task wasn't easy, but because of God, he accomplished it. God called Moses to deliver God's people from Egyptian bondage. Moses put his trust in the invisible God of the Bible, and God did not fail him. He led the people into the Promised Land because he leaned on God.

When life throws us a curveball and we can't see a solution, we must remember God can make the solution possible. When we have reached our limit and feel overwhelmed, we can remember what Paul said in Philippians 4:13: "I can do all things through Christ who strengthens me." We gain our strength from our dependence upon Jesus.

THOUGHT FOR THE DAY
Tasks that defy my capabilities shrink in size when I place my life in the hands of the Almighty. God makes it possible to overcome life's challenges when I depend on Him, abandoning my weak attempts in exchange for His strength and guidance.

PRAYER
Lord, I am weak, but You are strong. Help me place my trust and confidence in You only. With You, all things are possible. Thank You for all the times You have provided a way for me when it seemed impossible. You are a loving God Who is willing and able. In Jesus' name, amen.

Ordinary People

"And every man stood in his place all around the camp; and the whole army ran and cried out and fled" (Judges 7:21).

READ: JUDGES 7:2-25

God uses ordinary people to do extraordinary things. The person who is small in the eyes of others can accomplish the tasks of God. God uses ordinary people, despite their faults. Bigger is not always better in God's eyes.

God uses those who are willing to be used. He can use anyone He wants if that person is obedient. God provides all we need to be victorious, but only if we obey. We welcome success when we answer God's call with faith and commitment. Half-hearted compromise brings failure. Our plan is never better than God's.

God will work through you. He is on your side when you put your trust in Him. God works among the faithful to accomplish His tasks. So, answer the call of God on your life with faith and obedience.

THOUGHT FOR THE DAY
God can use anyone He wants if that person is obedient.

PRAYER
Dear Lord, help me always trust You. I know Your plans are perfect. In Jesus' name, amen.

From Self-Pity to Success

"Blessed is the man Who walks not in the counsel of the ungodly, Nor stands in the path of sinners, Nor sits in the seat of the scornful; But his delight is in the law of the LORD, And in His law he meditates day and night" (Psalm 1:1-2).

READ: PSALM 1:1-6

The young man drove his family from the foothills of the Ozarks to the California coast, seeking his fortune. Despair had driven him from his home to the promise of prosperity in a place that held high hopes and relief from economic hardship. Arriving in California with nothing to his name, he looked for a job to provide for his family's needs. Sadly, he found no one would hire an inexperienced and untrained migrant. Self-pity set in. His future appeared grim, yet he determined to try one more time. Sensing the Lord's direction, he approached a building contractor who was willing to offer him a job, but getting the job required him to hang a door on a new home's interior wall. Although he had never held a hammer, he tried his best. When he had finished, his boss said, "Well, I see you can't hang a door, but you're hired."

The young man garnered a great deal of experience as a carpenter and, with years of experience, became a successful builder on the West Coast. Isn't it just like God to offer hope when all hope has vanished? When life doesn't deliver the goods, our failures come home to haunt us, leaving us filled with doubt and self-pity. When our expectations are shattered, loss takes a toll on us. When we're void of all hope, the Lord provides. When we draw from His waters, He commands the circumstances. We may wallow in self-pity, but when we open our hearts to His will, we'll find provision, peace, and security.

THOUGHT FOR THE DAY

I'm reminded of God's provision when I'm immersed in my plans, driven by my efforts, propelled by self, and haven't achieved what I planned to accomplish.

PRAYER

"Lord, my aim is success on Your terms. Help me place my life in the center of Your will so that I might delight in You. In Jesus' name, amen.

The Gift Sale

"For by grace you have been saved through faith, and that not of yourselves; it is the gift of God" (Eph. 2:8).

READ: EPHESIANS 2:8-9

An email from a retailer listed items on sale: jewelry, clothing, decor. I love getting gifts, but I love giving gifts even more, so this captured my attention. This sale was a treasure trove filled with an abundance of possibilities. I anticipated what gems awaited me. I have a closet assigned as my "gift closet" for future gifts to friends and family. The Bible says in Acts 20:35, "I have shown you in every way, by laboring like this, that you must support the weak. And remember the words of the Lord Jesus, that He said, 'It is more blessed to give than to receive.'"

Giving will make us happier. Our Heavenly Father knows that core value more than we ever could. He gave His only begotten Son—the ultimate Gift—to save us. And His gift is free—no hidden charges. Salvation is an incredible gift. What an awesome God. What a Giver. What an amazing gift.

THOUGHT FOR THE DAY
God gave so that we might live eternally with Him.

PRAYER
Lord, help me be more like You. I want to give others the opportunity of knowing You and Your incredible gift of Jesus Christ to a world in need of a Savior. Thank You for choosing me to receive this gift. In Jesus' name, amen.

Copy-Cat Behavior

"Now therefore, please be careful not to drink wine or similar *drink, and not to eat anything unclean"* *(Judges 13:4).*

READ: JUDGES 13:1–8

Witnesses on the playground saw a mother force her four-year-old son to drink a bottle of beer. Police arrived and took the boy and his ten-month-old sister to the hospital. The boy tested positive for alcohol, and his sister showed cocaine in her system. The mother said she fed her son a bottle of beer every day. However, she couldn't understand why the baby girl tested positive for cocaine since she didn't breastfeed her.

Manoah's wife was barren, but the angel of the Lord appeared to her and told her she would have a son. The angel instructed her on what and what not to do. She was not to use alcohol. Nor was she to eat anything unclean. These were simple, clear-cut instructions that would keep her and the baby from harm. Manoah's wife followed the instructions and birthed a special baby boy named Samson.

Parents today would do well to follow the angel's instructions by ridding their homes of alcoholic beverages and anything else that would tempt them and their children.

THOUGHT FOR THE DAY
My children imitate what they see me do.

PRAYER
Lord, never allow me to be a stumbling block to my children. May I live a holy life, acceptable to You. Remind me my life is an example to my children. In Jesus' name, amen.

The Power of One

"That the man of God may be complete, thoroughly equipped for every good work" (2 Tim. 3:17).

READ: 2 TIMOTHY 3:16-17

Who might be the most powerful person in the world? Would it be the person who controls the economy? Or the person who maintains the dictates of the internet? What about the farmers who grow the crops we eat? Perhaps, it is the president of a nation.

While all the above wield power, they do not have absolute power. They might even seem anemic or weak when compared to the power of the Lord God Almighty. God reigns with omnipotent power. He is the Supreme Power over all and in all.

A person doesn't have to earn a doctorate or have a vast array of wealth to own a portion of power. We merely need the transcending power of God. Moses is one example. He worked with God to bring ten plagues to Egypt. He then led the Israelites out of bondage. Later, the Hebrew children fought the battle of Jericho and saw the walls fall when they obeyed God's mandates. In another miraculous circumstance, Samson called on God's power to avenge the Philistines, who were God's enemies. He destroyed the two pillars of the house where he stood, killing the occupants.

The disciples demonstrated the power of God in various situations. Peter was so full of the Holy Spirit that people brought the sick into the streets and laid them on beds so that his shadow might fall on them. A young boy with five barley loaves and two fish gave them to Jesus, Who gave them to the disciples and fed five thousand men, plus women and children. We can still tap into that Divine power when we trust God and act in faith. Jesus said in Matthew 17:20, "So Jesus said to them, 'Because of your unbelief; for assuredly, I say to you, if you have faith as a mustard seed, you will say to this mountain, *Move from here to there*, and it will move; and nothing will be impossible for you.'"

THOUGHT FOR THE DAY

The power of God belongs to the believer who extends their belief and refuses to limit God to the ordinary. Nothing is impossible for God or the person who believes in the unlimited power and ability of the great God, I Am. God fuels the passion of each one of us when we join Him and arrange our wills to coincide with His.

PRAYER

Lord, I humbly ask You to supply my faith to believe in and extend itself to Your unlimited love, knowing You and You alone are sufficient. You are more than enough. In Jesus' name, amen.

Connections with God

"Praying always with all prayer and supplication in the Spirit, being watchful to this end with all perseverance and supplication for all the saints" (Eph. 6:18).

READ: EPHESIANS 6:18-20

A young boy was on a far-away vacation with his elderly grandfather. His parents knew he was in responsible hands, but they longed to hear from him—to be reassured he was happy and comfortable. His parents relaxed when he called, telling them how happy he was.

The same holds true between God and us. We need to keep the connection flowing by communicating with our Heavenly Father. He never tires of hearing from His children. Prayer keeps the lines open. God wants us to pray without ceasing, to pray as if our life depended on it, and to pray as if others' lives depended on it. Because it does, we all need prayer.

But when should we stop praying? When we don't see needs met? When we receive our first miracle? Neither. We should never stop praying. Praying is our communication with a wonderful and loving Heavenly Father. He knows our needs, yet He longs to hear from us. Prayer reassures us we have open communication and a loving connection with Almighty God.

Pray to the Father and never say, "It's enough." God hears and cares. Keep the connection open. Continue praying, giving thanks, and addressing God with honor and praise as you make petitions to Him.

THOUGHT FOR THE DAY

Keep open connections between you and the Lord. He never tires of us coming to Him in prayer and thanksgiving.

PRAYER

Lord, my relationship with You depends on my connection to You through prayer. May I ever stay in sync with You through my prayers as I seek Your will. In Jesus' name, amen.

God Doesn't Make Junk

"For You have made him a little lower than the angels, And You have crowned him with glory and honor" (Psalm 8:5).

READ: PSALM 8:3-8

Have you ever heard the expression, "One man's trash is another man's treasure?" The saying often comes true when we go to a garage sale and purchase someone else's unwanted items. Sometimes, it feels as if we hit the jackpot. We have a purpose for our find and know just exactly what we plan to do with it. We recycle what is unwanted—bringing it to our home and possibly making it the crown jewel of our décor. When it is a genuine bargain, we cherish it even more.

God considers us His treasure. He doesn't make trash. Although we may feel unwanted, unnecessary, and unclaimed, Jesus paid a high price for us. We are valuable because He made us in His image.

Several years ago, a movie character referred to his son as "Mini Me." We might be loosely described as the same as our Creator. With some characteristics of the Divine, we come closer to drawing on His nature when we do His will and exhibit the fruits of the Spirit—love, joy, peace, longsuffering, kindness, goodness, faithfulness, gentleness, and self-control. Yes, we often fail to exemplify God's nature and display our sinful nature, but even then, God values us. His love extends to His entire creation.

THOUGHT FOR THE DAY
God loves me so much that He gave His only Son so that I can spend eternity with Him if I receive the gift of His Son.

PRAYER
Lord, thank You for loving me so extensively. Even when I fail and consider myself unworthy, You see my value. In Jesus' name, amen.

Love Without Limits

"Love never fails. But whether there are *prophecies, they will fail; whether* there are *tongues, they will cease; whether* there is *knowledge, it will vanish away" (1 Cor. 13:8).*

READ: 1 CORINTHIANS 13:1-13

Ordinarily, a mother's love is the greatest. Yet we can also observe love in nature and the human spirit. When we look at the mother bird feeding her baby bird a freshly harvested worm, we observe love. We also see love when we observe a mother bear protecting her cubs. And a mother nurturing her child through sickness, providing during all occasions, and supplying support throughout life shows human love.

But the ultimate love is God's love for His creation. Regardless of our age, income, or IQ, the Lord sees us as a person worth loving. We read in Genesis 1:26, "Then God said, 'Let Us make man in Our image, according to Our likeness." In Genesis 1:31, we read, "Then God saw everything that He had made, and indeed *it was* very good." God's love extends far beyond anything we can imagine. In a spiritual sense, His love would be endless, infinite, and eternal.

God's endless love enveloped humanity from the beginning of the ages. He developed His plan for salvation before Adam and Eve sinned in the garden. His love provided for anything that we might conjure up and do wrong. Most importantly, His plan included our redemption through Jesus.

God's love is infinite. He places no restrictions on who He will save. When we draw near to Him, He will draw near to us. We are all included in His loving, all-encompassing acceptance when we seek Him. God's love is eternal. His love reaches the furthest moment in time and then continues.

THOUGHT FOR THE DAY
The love of God has no limits.

PRAYER
God, help me to see Your infinite love. Surround me with Your love and acceptance as I draw near to You. In Jesus' name, amen.

Blessed to Bless Others

"The Lord bless you and keep you" (Num. 6:24).

READ: NUMBERS 6:22-27

A popular game show in the 1950s was *Queen For a Day*. Each contestant shared their stories with the audience. The winner who had the most heart-touching story was selected. The person who won the title of queen received gifts galore.

James 1:17 says, "Every good gift and every perfect gift is from above, and comes down from the Father of lights, with whom there is no variation or shadow of turning." As a child of God, we are free to live in the abundance of His blessings each day. Numbers 6:24-26 states, "The Lord bless you and keep you; The Lord make His face shine upon you And be gracious to you; The Lord lift up His countenance upon you And give you peace."

Recognizing that God is the Giver of all good gifts, we should thank Him for His goodness and blessings. Beyond that, we should share our blessings with others. We are blessed to be a blessing. If we fail to share the riches God has given us, we become like the Dead Sea: stagnant.

The Bible promises that if we give, we will receive. Let God flow through you. Give to others as God gives to you. Continue the flow by offering gifts and treasures.

THOUGHT FOR THE DAY
We are blessed to be a blessing.

PRAYER
Lord, thank You for blessing me. May I, in turn, bless others. In Jesus' name, amen.

Poverty or Provision

"For you know the grace of our Lord Jesus Christ, that though He was rich, yet for your sakes He became poor, that you through His poverty might become rich" (2 Cor. 8:9).

READ: 2 CORINTHIANS 8:7-14

Buck, the cow dog, lived on the farm. He was lanky and enjoyed lounging around the barnyard, just doing nothing. Buck was well-provided for, but his owners did not require much of him. He ate table scraps from his master's table and slept a lot. Then, one warm summer night, his master threw out some leftover corn cobs and the leftovers from dinner. Buck rushed to the scraps and devoured the tasty pork chop bones and baked beans, but he disregarded the corn cobs. They lay under the giant oak tree for days. Then, one day, a stray dog strolled up to the barnyard. He spied the corn cobs and grabbed one for himself. Buck suddenly got interested and grabbed the corn cob from his mouth. The corn cob was a prized trophy.

Just as Buck became interested in the corn cob when he saw another dog wanted it, some people desire what others have. They try to keep up with the Joneses. The cars others drive are the cars they want. The clothes others own are the ones they want to wear. They want to own a house in a particular neighborhood.

Jesus gave up the riches of Heaven for the poverty of earth. He became poor, so we might be rich in faith, truth, knowledge, and love. We may not wear designer labels, live in an elite neighborhood, or drive an expensive car; but the Lord provides for our material and spiritual needs when we place our trust in Him. His provision is our gift. He provides for us so that we will not be impoverished. His death on the cross secured our salvation. He promises us eternal life when we believe in His death, burial, and resurrection. This is His gift to us.

THOUGHT FOR THE DAY
Jesus did it all for us. He gave up Heaven's wealth so that we might have eternal life.

PRAYER
Lord, thank You for Your provision. I am eternally grateful that You were willing to give Your life so that I might have the hope of Heaven. In Jesus' name, amen.

Our Best Reward

"And I heard a loud voice from heaven saying, 'Behold, the tabernacle of God is with men, and He will dwell with them, and they shall be His people. God Himself will be with them and be their God'" (Rev. 21:3).

READ: REVELATION 21:1-7

Our family vacation promised golden sunsets, towering waterfalls, and fresh fruit whenever we wished. Our destiny to a beautiful South Pacific island offered a paradise even more impressive than the travel agent could portray. It couldn't have been more spectacular if it had been gilded in gold. The sounds of the ocean crashing, the tastes of exotic fruit, and the beauty of the fertile landscape exceeded our most lavish expectations. We savored our tropical paradise to the fullest. Finally, exhausted from our adventures, we were ready to head home. There's no place like home.

We who are in Christ are awaiting our new heavenly home. Revelation 21:1-2 describes our new home: "Now I saw a new heaven and a new earth, for the first heaven and the first earth had passed away. Also, there was no more sea. Then I, John, saw the holy city, New Jerusalem, coming down out of heaven from God, prepared as a bride adorned for her husband." Sounds wonderful, doesn't it.

We also read in Revelation 21:4-5, "And God will wipe away every tear from their eyes; there shall be no more death, nor sorrow, nor crying. There shall be no more pain, for the former things have passed away. Then He who sat on the throne said, 'Behold, I make all things new.' And He said to me, 'Write, for these words are true and faithful.'" A genuine paradise awaits us. No sorrow, no pain, no death, no crying. Reading on in Revelation 21:23, we learn that "the city had no need of the sun or of the moon to shine in it, for the glory of God illuminated it. The Lamb *is* its light." God's glory will outshine the moon, stars, and sun in our new home. The best part of going home is being with God. "He who overcomes shall inherit all things, and I will be his God and he shall be My son" (Rev. 21:7).

THOUGHT FOR THE DAY
Many wonderful riches await us in our heavenly home, but the greatest blessing is resting in God's presence.

PRAYER
Lord, help me live a life pleasing to You so that I will be ready for my new home. My best reward is going home. In Jesus' name, amen.

A Time for Every Purpose

"To everything there is a season, A time for every purpose under heaven" (Eccl. 3:1).

READ: ECCLESIASTES 3:1-8

In the South, tomatoes flourish during summer. They grow best when the hot sun beats down on them. Cooler weather strains them, and they don't do as well. Colder climates may damage or even destroy them.

On the other hand, pansies and kale do best in crisp, cool weather. Too much heat makes them wither. So, the pretty, little pansy turns its head down, as if embarrassed when the sun blasts its hot rays toward earth.

Different seasons are kinder to some plants and animal life according to the God-ordained nature He gives to each. For example, the polar bear loves the icy, cold Arctic, while the alligator prefers the warmth of the Florida everglades.

We also prefer different seasons. Some like it warm, while others enjoy the cooler weather. And it is God Who created the various seasons and adapted the different species to each. The writer of Ecclesiastes said there is "a time to every purpose" and a season for everything. God "made everything beautiful in its time" (Eccl. 3:11).

Some jobs are more seasonal than others. For example, pools need lifeguards during the summer when people are swimming, but lifeguards may find themselves unemployed in cold weather. On the other hand, ski instructors are in demand when snow covers the slopes.

One component, however, should prevail year-round, regardless of the weather: our commitment to the Lord. The fair-weather friend meets the foul-weather friend and joins them with a heart and mind turned toward God to greet whatever life delivers. No season is off-limits when it comes to accepting and serving the Lord. We must respond to His call whenever the Holy Spirit draws us to Him. In season and out, an eager and ready response to the Lord's bidding is vital for a close walk with Him.

THOUGHT FOR THE DAY
To live for God requires my willingness to follow Him in all circumstances—when conditions are good and things are unfavorable.

PRAYER
Lord, help me live for You at all times. Make me willing to do Your will regardless of the circumstances. In Jesus' name, amen.

Showing Mercy

"Blessed are the merciful, For they shall obtain mercy" (Matt. 5:7).

READ: MATTHEW 5:7-9

Mercy may not be tangible, but it is valuable. On some occasions, it is a gift worth more than gold. We find an example of this matchless mercy in Philippians 2:27: "For indeed he was sick almost unto death; but God had mercy on him, and not only on him but on me also, lest I should have sorrow upon sorrow." Who could argue that Divine healing is priceless? When doctors have done everything possible, and we are at the end of our rope, Divine healing is a gift of mercy from the Lord. This form of compassion is beyond measure; no human effort can match it.

We encounter opportunities to express mercy to people in all areas of life. When we go easy on someone who has wronged us, it cushions the edges of a strained relationship. Instead of harsh words and unkind deeds, we extend compassion, allowing the hurt to heal.

The person we have extended mercy to may return the favor by showing us kindness. Jesus said the merciful person would obtain mercy. We are blessed as we bless.

THOUGHT FOR THE DAY
Giving allows me to get. This precious gift of mercy benefits all.

PRAYER
Lord, if I want Your mercy, I must give mercy. Therefore, help me be generous with my mercy offerings to others. In Jesus' name, amen.

Negotiator

"Blessed are the peacemakers, for they shall be called the sons of God" (Matt. 5:9).

READ: MATTHEW 5:8-9

A comical song by Allan Sherman and Lou Busch called "Camp Granada" begins with the sender telling his parents he will enjoy camp more if it would stop raining. The song continues with the young boy bewailing the poison ivy and alligators while away from home.

But in 1978, at Camp David, located in the Catoctin Mountains in Maryland, President Jimmy Carter forged a peace treaty between Egypt and Israel. As the negotiator for this peace accord, President Carter acted as the peacemaker who implemented the peace process.

Jesus called peacemakers the sons of God. We don't have to be president of a country to be a peacemaker. Anyone who negotiates peace between two parties in conflict is a peacemaker. Peacemakers are worth their weight in gold, whether they negotiate a ceasefire or demilitarization between two countries or implement peace between a husband and wife. Peacemaker is a worthy title and one desirable by many. To be called a child of God merits a considerable degree of favor. God prizes the peacemakers. Being one is an honor worth the risk.

THOUGHT FOR THE DAY
A peacemaker resolves conflicts that might otherwise be catastrophic.

PRAYER
Lord, let me be a peacemaker, not a troublemaker, so that I, too, might be among those You call Your children. In Jesus' name, amen.

God's Reputation

"For the LORD is good; His mercy is everlasting, And his truth endures to all generations" (Psalm 100:5).

READ: PSALM 103:1-17; PSALM 100:5

God's reputation reaches beyond our human imagination. Among His traits are mercy, grace, love, and kindness. Also included are forgiveness, healing, compassion, redemption, and righteousness. We witness many of these character traits daily as God's reputation unveils itself to us.

We witness the mercy of God when we have wronged someone, yet God withholds His judgment. Instead, we receive His mercy and grace. Psalm 103:8 says, "The LORD *is* merciful and gracious, Slow to anger, and abounding in mercy."

When we ask God for forgiveness, we receive it. Psalm 103:10 promises, "He has not dealt with us according to our sins, Nor punished us according to our iniquities." God's love is everlasting. John 3:16-17 says, "For God so loved the world, that He gave His only begotten Son, that whoever believes in Him should not perish but have everlasting life. For God did not send his Son into the world to condemn the world, but that the world through Him might be saved."

God's love provides redemption from our sinful nature through the blood of Christ. God expresses His kindness through His gift of salvation to corrupt people who deserve punishment. Instead, we receive a reward of eternal life. God also gives some physical healing in addition to their spiritual healing. 1 Peter 2:24 says, "Who Himself bore our sins in His own body on the tree, that we having died to sins, might live for righteousness—by whose stripes you were healed."

Lamentations 3:22 says of God's compassion, "Through the LORD's mercies we are not consumed, Because His compassions fail not." And 1 Samuel 2:2 proclaims, "No one is holy like the LORD, For *there is* none besides You. Nor *is there* any rock like our God." Because God is holy, He also tells us to be holy (Lev. 11:45).

THOUGHT FOR THE DAY
God is great and awesome and clothed with honor and majesty. His glory extends throughout the earth and stretches across the heavens.

PRAYER
Lord, help me as I strive to imitate You. You have made me in Your image. Help me not to disappoint You by things I say or think. Instead, make me a vessel fashioned after You. I yield my life to You with a humble spirit, knowing You are supreme and almighty. In Jesus' name, amen.

Sweet Spot

"So I went to the angel and said to him, 'Give me the little book.' And he said to me, 'Take and eat it; and it will make your stomach bitter, but it will be as sweet as honey in your mouth'" (Rev. 10:9).

READ: REVELATION 10:5-11

Delicious drinks and desserts often hit our sweet spot. A tall glass of sweet tea makes pumpkin pie even more delectable. Moviegoers and home-theater enthusiasts also have a sweet spot where all the sounds come together and are located at the ideal distance from the visual screen, creating the optimal viewing experience. In tennis, racquetball, baseball, and golf, the sweet spot is where a combination of factors results in a more powerful hit when the player strikes the ball. Believers also have a sweet spot.

Revelation 21:1-7 describes the believer's sweet spot on a level that is out of this world:

Now I saw a new heaven and a new earth, for the first heaven and the first earth had passed away. Also there was no more sea. Then I, John, saw the holy city, New Jerusalem, coming down out of heaven from God, prepared as a bride adorned for her husband. And I heard a loud voice from heaven saying, "Behold, the tabernacle of God *is* with men, and He will dwell with them, and they shall be His people. God Himself will be with them and be their God. And God will wipe away every tear from their eyes; there shall be no more death, nor sorrow, nor crying. There shall be no more pain, for the former things have passed away." Then He who sat on the throne said, "Behold, I make all things new." And He said to me, "Write, for these words are true and faithful." And He said to me, "It is done! I am the Alpha and the Omega, the Beginning and the End. I will give of the fountain of the water of life freely to him who thirsts. He who overcomes shall inherit all things, and I will be his God and he shall be My son.

John's description is a precious and perfect scenario of the believer's future. We will receive an eternal home where God Almighty will dwell in His infinite love and mercy with His children. The ultimate sweet spot is not a place or a thing but a Person—Jesus Christ, Who is worthy to receive power, riches, wisdom, strength, honor, glory, and blessing. He is "the Alpha and the Omega, *the* Beginning and *the* End" (Rev. 22:13).

THOUGHT FOR THE DAY

The true sweet spot for the believer is our Savior, Who lives forever more. We shall be in perfect peace and enduring love when we see Him in our heavenly home.

PRAYER

Lord, may I be faithful as I yearn to meet You face-to-face and dwell with You eternally.
In Jesus' name, amen.

If Your Prayers Were a Song

"The LORD is my strength and song, And He has become my salvation; He is my God, and I will praise Him; My father's God, and I will exalt Him" (Exod. 15:2).

READ: EXODUS 15:1-2

Everybody has a litany of their favorite songs. My husband's favorite is John Denver's song, "Some Days Are Diamonds, (Some Days Are Stones)." Another favorite of his is "There Is a Fountain," a Gospel song proclaiming the goodness of God. One of my favorites is "Amazing Grace." For some, the Beatles' "Come Together," Elvis Presley's "Suspicious Minds," or "We Are the Champions" by Queen rank among the tops. Sometimes, couples claim a song as their song to play at their wedding.

Music affects our emotions, both positively and negatively. For many, music influences us and forms our identity. Music often indicates significant relationships, emotions, cultural, or political beliefs. And for Christians, music reaches the depths of devotion to God and our Savior.

Prayers can even be songs to the Lord. The book of Psalms is a collection of songs by various authors. What would your prayers consist of if you wrote them as songs to God? Would they be a song of praise, or would they be songs of distress? Would your prayers sound off a long list of wants, needs, or problems? Perhaps, your prayers would chant in a rhythmic staccato the failures and obstacles you've faced? Would your prayer life song contain a "to-do" list for God? Or would your prayers triumphantly sing of His enduring love and faithfulness?

Our prayers symbolically create music. Prayers of thanksgiving and praise compose happy songs to the Lord. We produce deep, meaningful songs when we are sincere and trust in His unfailing love. And when problems come, songs of triumph arise when we lean on God. When we repent, our song of sorrow rises to Heaven, and God hears and forgives. The triumphant song of rejoicing erupts because God makes His presence known.

THOUGHT FOR THE DAY

My prayers make me what I am as I depend on the Lord. May I look to God and lift my prayers to Him as music. Create in me a clean spirit and produce in me a song of prayer.

PRAYER

Lord, we always have a top-ten hit on the charts when we lift our prayers to You. Thank You. In Jesus' name, amen.

Overcomer

"Saying, 'I am the Alpha and the Omega, the First and the Last,' and, 'What you see, write in a book and send it to the seven churches which are in Asia: to Ephesus, to Smyrna, to Pergamos, to Thyatira, to Sardis, to Philadelphia, and to Laodicea'" (Rev. 1:11).

READ: REVELATION 1:10-11; 2:7, 11, 17, 26, 28; 3:5, 12, 21

The athlete who wins a race is the one who overcomes the odds and finishes first. So, let's enumerate the rewards of the believers in Christ for those who overcome.

- We will eat from the tree of life in the Paradise of God.

- We will not be hurt by the second death

- We will eat the hidden manna and receive a white stone with a new name written on it, which no one knows but the one who receives it.

- We will receive power over the nations and the morning star.

- We will receive white garments.

- We will have our names confessed before the heavenly Father, and His angels will not blot out our name from the Book of Life.

- We will be made a pillar in the temple of God on which God will write our new name.

- We will be granted the right to sit with Christ on His throne.

Let us work toward the reward of the high calling so that we might be an overcomer and reap the rewards outlined in Scripture.

THOUGHT FOR THE DAY
The Lord is faithful and just to reward those who seek Him.

PRAYER
*Heavenly Father, I overcome by the blood of the Lamb and the word of my testimony.
In Jesus' name, amen.*

The Battle Belongs to the Lord

"And every man stood in his place all around the camp; and the whole army ran and cried out and fled" (Judges 7:21).

READ: JUDGES 7:1-21

China's military—the People's Liberation Army—is the world's largest military, with approximately three million members. They have developed high-powered lasers, particle-beam weapons, high-powered microwave weapons, and electromagnetic pulse weapons. In addition, their existing armored troops, air-defense troops, and soldier militias are a significant force.

Gideon, a military commander of the Old Testament, garnered his strategy for battle from the Lord. The Lord told him that his army was too big. Judges 7:2 says, "And the LORD said to Gideon, 'The people who are with you are too many for Me to give the Midianites into their hands, lest Israel claim glory for itself against Me, saying, My hand has saved me.'" This battle was the Lord's.

God whittled an army of thirty-two thousand to a mere three hundred men. He determined whom He would use by their method of drinking water from a river. God disqualified them if they lapped like a dog by kneeling to drink. He chose the three hundred who put their hands to their mouths to drink. This small band of men defeated the entire Midianite army.

When we attempt to win battles ourselves, utilizing our tactics and strategies, we forget the battle belongs to the Lord.

THOUGHT FOR THE DAY

All the schemes and devices I try to employ in defeating the enemy are simply child's play in God's sight.

PRAYER

Lord, help me rely on You to defeat the enemy of my soul. There's no improving upon Your plans. Lead me by the Holy Spirit in all my actions. In Jesus' name, amen.

Activities of God

"I will praise You, O LORD, with my whole heart; I will tell of all Your marvelous works" (Psalm 9:1).

READ: PSALM 9:1-16

Busy, busy, busy. Days are marked by busy activities, running here and there, catching up on the latest, and making the most of our allotted hours. But have you ever considered God's activities? What activities does He engage in? We know from the first verse of the Bible in Genesis 1:1, "In the beginning God created the heavens and the earth." God continued in creation mode by making everything else. Later in Genesis 1:27, we read, "So God created man in his *own* image, in the image of God He created him; male and female He created them." God formed us.

When God finished His work, He rested on the seventh day. Even His rest had a purpose as Genesis 2:3 explains, "Then God blessed the seventh day and sanctified it, because in it He rested from all his work which God had created and made." So, God's day of rest was not idle but sanctified, set apart from all the others. Later, God told individuals to rest on this day and keep it holy. God creates, and God rests.

God's activities are also evident in circumstances. Jesus healed while He walked the earth, and He still heals today. Miracles happen, as we see with the ten lepers Jesus healed. In Luke 17:15, we read, "And one of them, when he saw that he was healed, returned, and with a loud voice glorified God." We are not far from our miracle. We must reach to the Lord and have faith in the God of the past and the God of today.

God is also active in His Word. He spoke the Ten Commandments to Moses on Mount Sinai, giving us action words to live by so that we might please Him and show Him honor. John 1:1 says, "In the beginning was the Word, and the Word was with God, and the Word was God."

Finally, God works through people. He is active on earth when His people bear fruit. John 15:5 says, "I am the vine, you *are* the branches. He who abides in me, and I in him, bears much fruit; for without Me you can do nothing." We are God's hands outstretched to others.

THOUGHT FOR THE DAY
God is in the details, always acting on our behalf His wonders to perform.

PRAYER
Lord, make me a vessel, willing to do what I can and to trust in You for the remainder. May I abide in You, assured of Your active interest in my life and Divine love for me. In Jesus' name, amen.

Strategy

"By faith, the walls of Jericho fell down after they were encircled for seven days" (Heb. 11:30).

READ: JOSHUA 6:1-20; HEBREWS 11:30

Strategy is essential in football. Coaches and players plan and execute plays involving formations and whom they put on the field. A team can overpower their opponent and win the game with the right strategy.

Strategy is also a big part of winning in the spiritual realm. The children of Israel marched around Jericho for seven days. God planned the strategy for ultimate victory to conquer the city. The team players were the men of war and seven priests, and the Lord laid out the game plan. The priests were to carry trumpets made of rams' horns before the ark of the covenant, one trumpet for each man. God told the men to march around the city once a day for six days. On the seventh day, they were to circle it seven times. The army had a rear guard who followed the ark.

God instructed the people to remain quiet as a part of their strategy. Then, at a precise time, they were to shout. "So, the people shouted when *the priests* blew the trumpets. And it happened when the people heard the sound of the trumpets, and the people shouted with a great shout, that the wall fell down flat. Then the people went up into the city, every man straight before him, and they took the city" (Josh. 6:20). The city's walls mysteriously fell, but it was no mystery to Israel. They understood obedience to God always means victory.

We, too, can have victory when we follow God's plans. His plans are no mystery when we read His Word, pray for direction, stay sensitive to the Holy Spirit, and obey Him. We will become aware of His plans as we listen to His still, small voice. Victory is inevitable when we relinquish our will to the will of our Heavenly Father. And just as the walls of Jericho fell for the children of Israel, our enemies will fall to the will of God.

THOUGHT FOR THE DAY
We win life's battles when God lays out His Divine plans and we follow them.

PRAYER
Lord, help me lay down my dreams and schemes and submit to Your design. Make me willing to obey You even when I don't understand or see what is ahead. Lift the spiritual fog and make my path clear as I press on toward You, always trusting in You. In Jesus' name, amen.

Quick, Apply Prayer

"Hear my prayer, O LORD, And let my cry come to You. Do not hide Your face from me in the day of my trouble; Incline Your ear to me; In the day that I call, answer me speedily" (Psalm 102:1-2).

READ: PSALM 102:1-4

Searching for a recipe that would satisfy my sweet tooth, I came across an article entitled, "Quick, Apply Chocolate!" Chocolate seems to be the cure-all for the food most likely to satisfy our cravings for something sweet. We submerge our taste buds in the delectable morsels with lavish abandon.

Chocolate sends our taste buds on exotic vacations that thrill the senses like no other food. Gourmet chocolate or a simple candy bar seems to be a therapy for anxiety, restlessness, boredom, and celebration. At times, a mouthful of chocolate provides a culinary experience beyond the ordinary. Chocolate is the choice for many who desire sweets. A diet without an occasional bite of chocolate would reduce some to frustration or even tears.

In the religious arena, we should balance our diets with spiritual necessities that warrant a life dedicated to the Lord. Unfortunately, we often associate religion with rituals and habits performed from repetition. But a more sincere and deeper relationship is garnered from commitment to God and submission to the Holy Spirit. This relationship begins with prayer to the One Who created and maintains all. Prayer is communication; without communication, no relationship exists, whether between husband and wife, teacher and student, or employee and employer. To bridge the unknown, we must communicate our ideas to others. Without it, we can only assume the thoughts and opinions of others.

God also communicates with us through the Bible. We learn about His character and plans and understand His nature. We don't have to guess what He desires for us. The Bible gives clear instructions about how God wants us to live. The Bible is God talking to us, and prayer is us approaching Him.

THOUGHT FOR THE DAY
Communication is a two-way street for both the speaker and the listener.

PRAYER
Lord, tune my ears to listen to Your voice as You speak to me through the Bible. And make me willing to express myself to You through prayer. In Jesus; name, amen.

Being Real

"Beware of false prophets, who come to you in sheep's clothing, but inwardly they are ravenous wolves" (Matt. 7:15).

READ: MATTHEW 7:13-23

Little Red Riding Hood is the story of a little girl who takes a walk through the woods to her grandma's house. The big, bad wolf approaches the little girl in the woods as she takes her food basket to her grandma. He then rushes ahead of her to her grandma's house and disguises himself as her grandma. As Little Red Riding Hood enters, she mistakes the wolf lying in bed for her grandma. "What a big mouth you have," Little Red Riding Hood said. The hungry wolf grabbed her and said, "The better to eat you."

We understand the underlying danger in this fairytale: beware of the big, bad wolf. The wolf's deception created a stir for Little Red Riding Hood. The wolf duped her into thinking her sweet grandma was awaiting her basket of goodies. Instead, a deceitful wolf intercepted, aiming to devour her and the food.

Jesus tells us to beware of false prophets waiting to devour us spiritually. Pretenders who appear to offer spiritual guidance can ruin our walk with God by leading us astray. Some may make false claims; others may dilute the truth; and still, others may make claims that lead us to disappointment and unbelief. For example, a claim that God will make us wealthy, famous, and problem-free if we believe in Him is unrealistic. Negatives and positives encumber our life path—a balance between the good and the bad. In reality, we experience a wide range of history in our personal lives.

To the unsuspecting, the spiritual wolf at the door longs to destroy our foundational beliefs. Sometimes, in the name of tolerance, the Gospel is whitewashed with permissiveness or indulgence. The false teacher may sugarcoat the code of conduct outlined in the Bible without wishing to offend anyone. Scripture guides us to live a godly life. A thorough study of the Bible is the only way to live free of deception. In an age of eroding values, false teaching opens the door for deception. Do not allow the enemy of your soul to disguise himself in false teaching that ultimately leads you away from the Lord.

THOUGHT FOR THE DAY
An awareness of God's truths portrayed in Scripture prevents my deception.

PRAYER
Lord, save me from deception. Make me a true believer who keeps Your statutes. In Jesus' name, amen.

Don't Give Up

"Therefore, do not cast away your confidence, which has great reward. For you have need of endurance, so that after you have done the will of God, you may receive the promise" (Heb. 10:35-36).

READ: HEBREWS 10:35-38

Eubotas, an ancient Libyan athlete, was so sure of his victory in a running competition that he had his victory statue made before the race began. He won the race and dedicated the statue on the same day. Now, that is confidence.

Physical, emotional, and spiritual obstacles and struggles comprise our race and test our endurance. As the situations heat up, we may want to put things in reverse and quietly back out—or even slam on the brakes and quit. Maybe it seems impossible to go through the storm or get to the other side.

God doesn't want us to buckle under life's pressures but to move forward. God goes with us through the trials of life when we put our trust in Him. He will hold our hand and lead us through the roughest spots and the tender, rich experiences. He is there in every circumstance. God refines us through the tests and trials. Like the Little Engine That Could, we can say, "I think I can; I think I can; I think I can." We can do everything through Christ when we allow Him to move on our behalf.

When we have passed the tests of life with God at the helm, we will receive the promise of eternal life. It will be worth it all.

THOUGHT FOR THE DAY
Though the way seems rough at times, God is in the midst of it all.

PRAYER
Lord, I put my trust in You in good and bad times. Help me focus on You in whatever situation I find myself in. In Jesus' name, amen.

Beyond Our Expectations

"But as it is written: 'Eye has not seen, nor ear heard, Nor have entered into the heart of man The things which God has prepared for those who love Him'" (1 Cor. 2:9).

READ: 1 CORINTHIANS 2:9-11

"Feeling Lucky?" was the rant for the casino billboard. Enticing players to seek their fortune in casino money, the advertisement encouraged people to play their hands at winning—even if it meant using money they needed for car and house payments or food and utilities. But, often, the contender for the casino's fortune suffered a loss. After all, the casino's goal was to stay in business.

One thing we don't need to gamble with is our salvation and relationship with the Lord. Placing our lives in the hands of an all-loving God promises a secure future and untold riches. He offers abundant life to all who seek God and trust in Him. Material, spiritual, and emotional wealth await us on reaching our eternal home.

Some people have difficulty expressing their love for others, but not God. He desires to lavish riches on us that exhaust our imagination. We can't imagine what God has prepared for us in eternity. He will wipe away every tear and forgive every sin of those who love Him. Won't it be wonderful there?

THOUGHT FOR THE DAY
My wildest dreams can't imagine what God has planned for me.

PRAYER
Lord, help me stay focused on doing Your will and loving You. Thank You for the promise of Heaven where You surround those who love You with awesome gifts far beyond anything we can imagine. In Jesus' name, amen.

Finding Waldo

"And you will seek Me and find Me, when you search for Me with all your heart" (Jer. 29:13).

READ: JEREMIAH 29:10-14

"Where's Waldo" is a visual game where one must find Waldo, who camouflages himself in a picture of various graphics. The pictorial game may entertain fans for hours through different matching exercises, quizzes, doodles, and tangled-line teasers. The game tests a person's perseverance and patience. The detective work calls for concentration and focus. One sighting of Waldo causes celebration and success.

Jeremiah encourages God's people to seek and search for the Lord with all their hearts—nothing casual or faint-hearted. A comprehensive search for God results in finding Him, embracing His presence, and drawing near Him. This fervent searching develops a loving relationship with Him. God doesn't hide in impossible places beyond our reach. Instead, He longs to be found by those desiring a closer walk with Him. Prayer is one step toward success in finding God. Begin your search.

THOUGHT FOR THE DAY
Embedded in a deep desire to know the Lord, I find joy in His presence when I pray. The God of the universe is near when I seek Him wholeheartedly.

PRAYER
Lord, it is never too soon or late for me to search for You. So let me continue seeking You as I journey through life. Help me to immerse myself in You as I pray. In Jesus' name, amen.

Finishing Strong

"For the Son of Man will come in the glory of His Father with His angels, and then He will reward each according to his works" (Matt. 16:27).

READ: MATTHEW 16:24-27

"The Last Mile of the Way," written by Johnson Oatman in 1908, resounds with anticipation of reward from our Heavenly Father:

If I walk in the pathway of duty,

If I work till the close of the day,

I shall see the great King in His beauty,

When I've gone the last mile of the way.

We may struggle throughout our Christian walk, but our determination to live for the Lord—putting our trust and confidence in Him—will see us to a victorious end. Although we sometimes fail Him, we can pull ourselves up by our spiritual bootstraps—the bootstraps that connect us to the risen Lord—and win the race. The believer who finishes the race walking in the ways of the Lord gains much. Our reward is a heavenly home with our Savior.

When we fall, we reach out for God's strength; when we trespass, we seek His forgiveness; when we doubt, we remember His faithfulness. God's provision strengthens when we fail. Our life-walk with the Lord begins with a triumphant step when we anticipate the glory we shall see when we enter our heavenly home. God wants us to keep our eyes on Him; trust Him; obey His laws; and continue to love, worship, and serve Him. For those who finish strong, we long to see the great King in His beauty and bask in His presence. Until God reveals His great glory, we can only imagine His magnificence that awaits us.

THOUGHT FOR THE DAY
I will encounter many trials, but I can finish strong when I place my confidence and trust in God.

PRAYER
Lord, I long to experience the presence of Your glory, majesty, dominion, and power both now and forever. Help me finish strong. In Jesus' name, amen.

Mission Accomplished

"The last enemy that will be destroyed is death" (1 Cor. 15:26).

READ: 1 CORINTHIANS 15:24-28

"Mission Impossible," a television series during the late 1960s and early 1970s, portrayed secret government agents who received instructions on a recording that would then self-destruct. The theme song that followed drew the viewers into a dramatic setting where the undercover agent pursued the villain in a conflict of international proportions. The villain in this television series was covert and evil—often a powerful dictator or crime lord. Apprehending or destroying the target meant the secret agents faced constant danger and conflict.

As believers, we engage in heavy battle with the enemy of our soul, Satan. Ephesians 6:12 identifies the enemy: "For we do not wrestle against flesh and blood, but against principalities, against powers, against the rulers of the darkness of this age, against spiritual *hosts* of wickedness in the heavenly *places*."

But we do not have to be weak or fearful. Ephesians 6:10 says, "Finally, my brethren, be strong in the Lord and in the power of His might." We are equipped for battle when we place our trust in the Lord, rely on His strength, and dress in the whole armor of God. This armor provides protection. It includes the armor of truth, the breastplate of righteousness, the gospel of peace, the shield of faith, the helmet of salvation, and the sword of the Spirit, which is the Word of God (Eph. 6:14-17). We should always pray and watch until the end (Ephesians 6:18). We will accomplish our mission when our last enemy—death—is defeated.

THOUGHT FOR THE DAY
Engaged in a spiritual battle, I enjoy success when I put my trust in the Lord.

PRAYER
Lord, You are the Defender of my soul. Therefore, I place my hope and trust in You. In Jesus' name, amen.

Ambassador International's mission is to magnify the Lord Jesus Christ and promote His Gospel through the written word.

We believe through the publication of Christian literature, Jesus Christ and His Word will be exalted, believers will be strengthened in their walk with Him, and the lost will be directed to Jesus Christ as the only way of salvation.

For more information about
AMBASSADOR INTERNATIONAL
please visit:

www.ambassador-international.com

Thank you for reading this book. Please consider leaving us a review on your social media, favorite retailer's website, Goodreads or Bookbub, or our website.

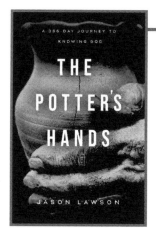

The day Jason Lawson's stress reached a tipping point, he found himself shaking so badly he couldn't even pour orange juice into a blender for his family's breakfast. He felt like his world was falling around him, and he was afraid of losing his family, his job, and his mind. But that was the day Jason met the Potter. That day, Jason began a journey with the Potter to learn Who He really is and why He created man, and this journey is compiled in his devotional *The Potter's Hands: A 366-Day Journey to Knowing God.*

Through fifty-two weekly devotionals, Martin Wiles uses his experiences and insights from hiking the Appalachian Trails to show the reader how to grow closer to the Lord.

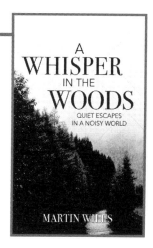

Faythelma Bechtel knows the tempest, but she also knows the One Who calms the storm. After losing two daughters and her husband, Faythelma has clung tighter to her Savior and longs to help others who are struggling to find peace in their own storms.

This devotional journal is not meant to be read as a daily plan, but instead offers meditations on Scripture to help for your unique circumstance.